Couch Time with Carolyn

Couch Time with Carolyn

A Memoir

Katie Hart Smith

To Judy —
Many
Blessings!
Katie H Smith

Maple Wood

Publishing

For more information and to make inquiries, visit www.katiehartsmith.com

10 9 8 7 6 5 4 3 2

Library of Congress Cataloging-in-Publication Data is available on file.

ISBN: 978-1-304-91616-7

Printed in the United States of America

Cover art by Susan Miller

Dedication

For Carolyn

&

The Dunwoody Girls

"And now abides faith, hope, love, these three; but the greatest of these is love."

1 Corinthians 13:13

Acknowledgements

I would like to bestow my heart-felt appreciation to the following people:

The Dunwoody Girls - Dorothy Sewell Kopp, Margaret Sewell Fulcher, Carole Sterrett Doner, Susan "Baynham" Miller, and Susie Lynn Shaver for your enduring friendship through the ages. You are a blessing in my life. I have loved working together on this project. This book reflects our love and joy for life.

My editor, Sallie Boyles, for your insight and guidance to help make this memoir special and authentic – one that tells the tale about a group of strong, southern, sassy women.

My husband, Jeff, for your love and support...always.

My furry, four-legged kids, Maggie, Baby Angus, and Augie, for being faithfully by my side to lend a paw or an ear as I wrote the manuscript.

CHAPTER 1

Prayers

My prayer just before turning thirty, nearly two decades ago

Dear God,

I am divorced, lost and afraid. I have forty dollars in my checking account and I pray that it will sustain me through the week. I pray that you will watch over me. Keep me safe from harm. Allow me to be your ever faithful servant. I am uncertain of what life has in store for me and if I'll ever find true love. Please bless and care for my family and friends. Forgive me for my sins. Please let me walk in your world for another day so that I can become the woman you created me to be.

Your faithful servant,

Katie

P. S. Go Dawgs!

In your name I pray. Amen.

Lawrenceville, Georgia, one year ago

Looking back, I realized the news would hit eventually, just not so soon. Tragedy was making an unscheduled visit today. It quietly crept in at a time when life couldn't be better.

Preparing to make dinner, I turned on the faucet and gazed out the kitchen sink window. That's when I first noticed the buds of spring in my backyard. Purple irises had popped up through the red clay. Scarlet buttons adorned the camellia bushes. Yellow jonquils bloomed in clusters down by the creek that ran beside the property line of the house. The vibrant colors had me in a trance until my cell phone vibrated loudly against the granite countertop and emitted a marimba ringtone, as if demanding my attention.

Was it six o'clock already?

Confirming the time, two black metal hands split the face of an enormous faux antique clock on the wall. (Like many of the Southern women I know, I appreciate a minimalist approach to decorating. Take me to a spa and I'm content to stare at a single conch shell all afternoon long while listening to the roar of waves of some distant seashore piped in from overhead speakers and inhaling the fresh clean aromas of lavender and clean linen. When in my personal surroundings, however, blank walls and bare furniture seem lacking, like a great outfit crying for a pop of jewelry and fabulous shoes. I prefer to look around and see the pieces I've collected, including the big, bold clock, that make a house a home.) Dorothy would be calling from her car, and whatever she had on her mind, I didn't want to miss it.

Moving swiftly, I used the back of my arm to shut off the water, then dried my hands on my pant legs and rushed over to the phone. Sure enough, *Dorothy* appeared on the caller I.D. Stuck in more stop than go traffic, she had a habit of returning her daily phone calls from family members and friends during her hour-long evening commute home to Lilburn from the downtown Atlanta investment firm where she worked.

"He-ey!" Her voice crackled through some static on the line.

Even without hearing the word clearly, I would have known she'd started the conversation with *hey*—something I had been reprogrammed to say instead of *hi* upon moving south of the Mason-Dixon Line to Georgia as a young kid. Not to be confused with the Northern form (Hey! I'm trying to get your attention!), the friendlier Southern version—a proper greeting and conversation starter—was essential lingo to survive in the South.

"Hey!" I echoed. "What's going on with you?" While listening, I opened the pantry to inventory the plethora of ingredients from which I'd ingeniously concoct a five-star dining experience for my husband Jeff. Hours of watching the Food Network had made me such a better cook—or at least Jeff thought so.

"Not much," Dorothy answered. In a blasé tone, she described her day at work and filled me in on the latest news about her husband Robert and daughter Jennifer. Dorothy reminded me that along with Jennifer, a high school senior this year, her nephew Brad, Margaret's son, was also graduating in June. Margaret, Dorothy's only and younger sister, resided in Killeen, Texas.

Gosh, how time flies, I thought. I couldn't believe that Jennifer, the precious and special girl I'd known all of her life, even before she was born, was graduating high school.

I reached for what I concluded would be the perfect foundation for our evening's healthy, gourmet meal—two packages of Ramen noodles and vegetable broth—and placed them on the kitchen counter. I then opened the refrigerator and rummaged through the hydrator for fresh herbs and vegetables. The peppery aroma of the fresh basil caught my attention, so I pulled out a few leaves, lifted them to my nose and inhaled deeply. *Hmmmm*. At least I could pretend to be a gourmet chef!

"Uh …" the timbre of Dorothy's voice had changed, causing me to put everything on hold, even my breath for a second. Sensing the news would be bad, I returned the basil into the hydrator, closed the refrigerator door, and leaned on the cold countertop. Pressing my cell phone even closer to my ear, I waited for Dorothy to speak the words.

"My mom's health has taken a bit of a turn for the worst."

"Go on," I said.

"Mom's test results show that her cancer has returned and spread into multiple organs."

Mom was *Carolyn* to me. She refused to be called Mrs. Sewell anymore since her daughter's friends, the only ones who ever addressed her by her formal name, were no longer kids. Carolyn said she was reserving Mrs. Sewell for Dorothy's grandma, the proper lady who had lived in Rome, Georgia. Dorothy's grandma had been a traditional Southern woman who expected everyone to use her formal name.

No matter how she insisted that I address her, Dorothy's mom was a second mother to me. We became fast and close friends in my young adult years. While in my thirties and forties, I spent countless hours at her house, confiding in her. I was divorced, lost, and struggling to pick up the pieces in order to rebuild and refashion myself into the woman I always dreamt, prayed and knew I could be. We also just loved to gab, laugh, and tell stories during that cathartic time, which I affectionately came to know as Couch Time with Carolyn.

As Dorothy's news began to hit me, I recalled sitting on the edge of Carolyn's yellow sofa in her den during one of our Couch Time with Carolyn sessions. It was the first time I ever heard her utter the c-word—*cancer*. Stunned, I listened to her explain that doctors found an abnormal lump in her breast that a biopsy confirmed was cancerous. The wake-up call told us that life could turn on a dime, without warning.

A lumpectomy of the affected breast, followed by chemotherapy drugs and radiation, had placed the disease in remission, but only temporarily. I listened as Dorothy rattled off a list of locations where the horrible cancer had invaded, including Carolyn's liver and lungs, as well as a few more areas of the body where the radiologist noticed spots.

"Oh, I am so sorry to hear this news, Dorothy," I uttered. My eyes welled with tears and my heart sank.

"The doctors give Mom," Dorothy began, her voice lowering to a whisper, "five more months."

Five more months to live and die. What do you do in that short amount of time? The countdown clock had started. Time was not on Carolyn's side. Snapping out of the fury of thoughts, I forced myself to focus on Dorothy's voice.

"Mom has decided not to seek any treatment," Dorothy offered. "She isn't a candidate for surgery."

Changes in Carolyn's health involving major medical issues surfaced soon after Dorothy's dad died on the operating table. He had suffered a major complication during open heart surgery at St. Joe's—or how we Atlantans familiarly refer to St. Joseph's Hospital.

Life had been a bit rough on Carolyn, who resiliently turned those bad cards she had been dealt into winning hands with style, complete with a sharp sense of humor. Carolyn was also decisive, not the kind of person who would let something like cancer tell her how to play out her final days. When it was time to fold, she would have some say about the terms.

"Is there anything I can do for either one of you?" I asked.

Still reeling from the news, I recalled my Georgia State University nursing training about death and dying. Mentally pulling away for a moment, I saw myself in a state of shock and denial, as explained by the Kübler-Ross model that I had to memorize. Although individuals processed grief differently, people tended to go through some or all of the same stages, sometimes in no particular order: 1) denial; 2) anger; 3) bargaining; 4) depression; and 5) acceptance. The length of time one spent in any given area could vary depending up on the person's coping skills.

I'm in stage one, I thought.

"No, not right now," Dorothy was saying. "I can't think of anything. Just keep her in your prayers."

"I sure will," I affirmed. "You both will be in my prayers."

After saying our good-byes, I went over to a dry erase board that hung behind the kitchen door. Finding a green marker in the drawer, I wrote Carolyn and Dorothy's names under the word *prayers*. I regularly updated my list as an everyday reminder to pray for those in need. Wasting no time, I lifted up my thoughts of Carolyn and Dorothy to the Lord.

Dorothy and I had first met, becoming fast friends, in the seventh grade at Shallowford Elementary school in a suburb northeast of Atlanta called Dunwoody. The year was 1976, our country's Bicentennial. The nation, full of patriotism and nostalgia, was celebrating the two-hundredth anniversary of the adoption of the Declaration of Independence. (In accordance, thanks to our mother, my younger sister Julie and I were dressed in a red, white and blue color palette every single day!) My father, who was working for a large pharmaceutical company, also had something to celebrate. He had received a promotion to head up the sales territory in the Southeast, so my family moved to Dunwoody, Georgia, from Richmond, Virginia, just in time to settle into our new home before the new school year began. I had to adjust right away to a thick Deep South accent and the powerful humidity, which could ruin a hairdo within five seconds of leaving my air conditioned house.

Moving from place to place, however, was not foreign to me; Dad was frequently transferred across the country at his employer's convenience. After being born in San Diego, California, during my father's service in the Navy, I had lived in Ohio twice, Indiana, New Jersey and Virginia before the age of eleven.

Although starting over in each new state and making new friends was rough, especially on the first day at a new elementary school, I welcomed a challenge. Besides, I wasn't shy, and I *loved* to talk. Consequently, I acclimated quickly to my new classrooms, teachers, and classmates, as evidenced by the "needs improvement" and "unsatisfactory" conduct comments on report cards. In preparation for my parents' predictable straighten-up-and-fly-right lecture, I'd muster my best doe-eyed innocent, I-have-no-idea-why-my-teacher-gave-me-that-mark-in-conduct look. They'd still lecture me until they were blue in the face, but no matter what, their quick-witted daughter with blue eyes, bowed legs, freckled nose and strawberry-blonde, lopsided pigtails refused to be a wallflower.

My personality perfectly paired with Dorothy's, as evidenced by thirty-five years of friendship. From the beginning, we were opposites who balanced each other out. As kids, for instance, she enjoyed following the rules, while I typically found a way to gently bend them. Even so, I could always find a way to crack her up in class when we were supposed to be quietly reading. Because she'd listen intently to the teacher's instructions, I'd have to seek out Dorothy for clarification each time I wasn't paying attention and missed the details. Clearly, she was left brain dominant and I enjoyed tapping into my creative right brain.

As I returned the marker to the drawer, the home phone rang. Seeing *Lawrenceville Police Department* on the caller I.D. would send most into a state of panic and concern, especially after just talking with a distraught friend who was driving. But I'm a police officer's wife. And Jeff, a captain for the local city police department, always called the home phone to tell me he was on his way. It was also his encrypted manner of telling me he was hungry and asking what was for dinner.

Aware of my closeness with Dorothy and of my special bond with Carolyn, he was genuinely saddened when I relayed the latest. At the same time, knowing he was usually my first priority, Jeff prepared to take a backseat as my friends and I, the self-proclaimed Dunwoody Girls (or DGs for short), sprang into action to be there for Dorothy and her family.

I opted not to tell him about the vegetarian concoction I'd planned for dinner. Dorothy's news was tragic enough.

CHAPTER 2

The Dunwoody Girls

The DGs were never superheroes. We were and always will be an ordinary group of five women who share an extraordinary friendship—one that began at Shallowford Elementary and continued through Dunwoody High School and into the present. Doing everything together, we were thick as thieves growing up and have remained inseparable as adults.

We are all the same age, but many of our similarities end there. Whatever universal forces brought us together—God, fate, angels—none of us are quite sure. We can say for certain it will never be undone.

Dorothy is the eldest of the group, by all of eight months, followed by Susie, Susan, me, and then Carole, the youngest. The idea of growing one year older was never a big deal, except that birthdays were causes for celebrating together from the time we were still young enough to fit individual candles on our cakes. When we became young adults, the milestones did take on a deeper meaning—special celebrations of life, love and friendship. The significance of all that our friendship represented continued to grow as we turned the big 3-0 and the big 4-0, and, inevitably, as we have entered the decades when our candles must be limited to prevent an infernal blanket of molten wax from engulfing a sheet cake.

The DGs' friendship includes parents, all of whom have been close with one other and with us. As kids, we spent every day at school and almost every weekend together, and we were all raised by the same moral compasses. Faith, family and friends were our foundation, although our denominations are different: I'm Methodist; Dorothy, Baptist; Carole, Lutheran; Susan, Presbyterian. Although Catholic, Susie and Dorothy spent Wednesday nights and Sundays at Dunwoody Methodist Church with me since we were members of the youth choir. When we were too young to drive, our moms took turns chauffeuring us to choir practice and all over town—to the mall, the movie theater, the ice skating rink, and high school football games. Therefore, while you won't find a family tree linking all of our kin folk together, the compilation of photos taken of all of us over the years proves otherwise. We have long acted and behaved more like sisters than friends.

Growing up, we lived in a middle-class subdivision of colonial-style homes in a family-oriented community. My home, the Hart house, was the hub for all DG festivities, and my parents loved having all of the girls over.

Mom, making herself five feet, four inches tall by teasing her frosted brown hair and wearing her wedge shoes, adored any opportunity to entertain us by organizing activities and crafts. One way she regularly amused us (and probably convinced the DGs we were Greek) was by dancing through the kitchen swirling a linen dish towel over her head to clear smoke, showing us how the smoke alarm could also be used as a cooking timer!

Often mistaken in public for some famous person of the day, typically Arnold Palmer, Chevy Chase, or a Congressman or Senator, Dad is the musically talented, piano playing, comedian of the bunch who has kept us in stiches. To this day, Susan, always the last person to let her emotions loose, develops an eating disorder when she visits with my parents: Thanks to uncontrollable laughter, she can't sit at a table with my Dad without spewing food from her mouth or a liquid substance from her nose.

Although a tight group, the five of us were never affiliated with any particular clique at school. The DGs were friends with everyone. Peers and adults alike also considered us the good girls, but we weren't above getting into some mischief. During one of many high school spend-the-night parties at my house, the DGs decided to shatter the good girl stereotype by "rolling" a random house in our subdivision. This was a total stretch for us, but no one backed out; everyone arrived at the sleepover armed and ready with a roll of toilet paper. We probably carried our premeditated guilt on our faces, giving our parents a pretty good inkling of what we were doing, but only Carole's cost conscious father expressed an objection—to the waste. He allowed her to take one roll to the slumber party on one condition: She had to promise to bring it back in its entirety!

Around midnight, after downing many slices of pizza and drowning ourselves in Coke, we headed off into the darkness. Hyped up on adrenaline and sugar, with toilet paper in hand, we set our sights on houses in the next cul-de-sac. We were silently making our way down the street, our hearts already beating wildly, when we heard quick steps coming toward us in the night. Suddenly, the person was running. The DGs panicked. Clutching our rolls, we scattered, diving into azalea bushes and darting behind cars.

"Katie.... Katie.... Katie...." Mom's voice whispered through the darkness.

Completely dumbfounded, I stood, emerging from the shadows. Moving to an area of brightness from a streetlight, I whispered, "Mom? Is that you? What are you doing out here? I thought you were sleeping!"

She was dressed all in black—black sweater top; black chino pants; black wedge shoes. In her mind, she was perfectly outfitted for the occasion. I caught a whiff of her Chanel Number 5 perfume in the midnight air and observed that she was also wearing her favorite coral-colored frosted lipstick. Noting the absence of her signature pearl necklace, I assumed that mom had chosen to leave the strand at home on the dresser. After all, a clandestine outdoor activity called for inconspicuous attire!

"I overheard your plan," she confessed. "I thought it best to be out here with you … you know, in case you all got caught. At least you'd be caught in the act … you know … with your mother. If you got into trouble, I might as well be in trouble with you, too. You know … as the adult of the group." She put a lot of emphasis on "adult" as she, too, wielded a roll of two-ply in her hands.

"What? Oh, my! Are you kidding me?" My immediate response was so conflicted. Mom's appearance in contrast to ours—none of the DGs were dressed in all black—made me realize we had overlooked an important element. I didn't know if I should be mortified because I wasn't sporting the right outfit, furious in the sense that my mom needed a good scolding for not acting like a proper parent, or relieved and joyful that she had tapped into her inner child. I chose the last emotion.

Bewildered but also relieved to learn that the footsteps had belonged to Mrs. Hart, the DGs surfaced from their hiding places, accepting that Mom would join us in rolling an unsuspecting neighbor's house. She earned the "Coolest Mom on the Planet" award on that night of broken rules and shattered stereotypes.

With countless coming-of-age experiences to bond us, we naturally continued our friendship into our adult years. Logistics helped. And as life would have it, four DGs ended up residing in Gwinnett County (one of Georgia's fastest growing areas about twenty-five miles northeast of downtown Atlanta) with only a fifteen-minute drive to separate us. In the rare event that traffic wasn't heavy on I-85 south, we were just thirty minutes away from Susan, who had returned to Dunwoody to raise her family.

If a catastrophe of any size struck one of the sisters, the DGs' phone tree would be activated faster than a 9-1-1 dispatch operator could notify the fire and police departments of an emergency. As the life crisis response team, we each fell into our respective roles depending upon the situation.

Carole and Susie, both elementary school teachers, have always done an excellent job of transmitting messages, giving orders, and providing and following directions with the best generals in command at West Point.

With big blue eyes that enhance her round, friendly face and ready smile, Carole is the classic extrovert. Her contagious, deep, hearty laugh makes her one of the most fun loving of our group. Also a charitable soul with a rich spirit, she is a lifelong, active member of her Lutheran church. At the same time, she's always in complete control and runs a tight ship in her classroom and at home. Even her pantry items are categorized and organized so that labels face out on the shelves in her kitchen, and each and every Tupperware container has its perfectly matched lid. Carole further takes after her frugal father, refusing to waste a penny, let alone a full roll of toilet paper.

In striking contrast to Carole, Susie is carefree with her finances. Without a doubt, she marches to the beat of her own drum. Organizational skills are not her forte. Dollars bills, change and mail can be found stuffed into a variety of drawers and strewn across the floors of her car, bedroom and kitchen. Despite her short stature of four feet, nine inches and cherubic face with a perpetual blush, she can command attention from the most chaotic kindergarten class, thanks to her booming voice. Chronic inner ear issues left her with a hearing loss, and at times her vocal decibel levels fluctuate from a whisper to a startling volume. We also take notice of Susie because we can count on her for honest, insightful, loving and unfiltered opinions. Rather unpredictably, she developed a small, defined comfort zone over the years and, as a result, has become the most tentative, anxious and inhibited one of the bunch.

Susan, whom we have affectionately (and typically) referred to as Baynham, her maiden name, since high school, has a stoic, no-nonsense manner that is well suited to her corporate position with a big telecommunications company. As one who wants only the facts in bulleted form, no fluff or long-winded stories, she prefers to keep most conversations short, sweet and to the point. Seeing her fall apart in public is rare. I believe the DGs have witnessed tears stream from her green eyes just twice in her life: first when her cat General died and then at her grandma's funeral. Given that stoic demeanor of hers, Susan lends a strong shoulder to cry on. We also admire how smart, punctual and structured she is, but that's not all. She lets her blonde hair down, especially when she taps into her creative side with crafts and DIY projects.

Dorothy and I are the take-charge caregivers, and the roles come naturally to us both. We are the ones to gather the troops, lay out the strategy and implement the tactics. The other DGs never have to question who will compile the task list, check off each item as it is completed, and get the job done right the first time.

Dorothy, the old soul of the group, wears her thick, dark brown, highlighted hair in short layers cropped around her ears. The no-nonsense cut is perfectly suited for her role in financial investments and portfolio management, an arena historically dominated by men. Glasses frame her hazel-blue eyes and further complement her look as an analytical thinker. Dorothy always has perfectly manicured hands and toes, which not only reflect her attention to detail, but also accentuate her graceful fingers and petite feet. Additionally, more meaningful than her looks, her charming smile and graceful laugh convey a sense of immediate trust, confidence and comfort to those around her.

I am wired for crisis management. The nursing training taught me to remain calm, composed and consciously aware of my surroundings during an emergency, and while many people claim to welcome a challenge, I really do. I'll pause long enough to assess the situation from different angles and then put my spin on the situation. I'm in my glory when a problem begs for an original way around it, but beyond ideas, I believe in an itemized strategy with action items. Under all conditions, I am a Southern woman who embraces the concept of making some kind of effort to look great. Like my mother, I have a flair for fashion, so my hair length and style, and my nail color change with my moods. Like my father, I also have the tendency to tap into my inner smartass when the moment allows; furthermore, I wholeheartedly believe that doses of laughter are medicinally necessary to help relieve stress in tense situations.

Together, we have walked down many aisles for the milestones—graduations, weddings and funerals. From sharing in the joys and comforting each other during times of sorrow, we knew upon hearing about Carolyn that we would once again converge and activate our DG powers. Dorothy needed us. Carolyn needed us.

This life event had summoned the DG sisterhood, and we were reporting for duty.

CHAPTER 3
Couch Time and Mother's Helper

Choosing among all of the DG parents, I was the closest to Dorothy's mom, thanks to a special bond that we forged when I became a young adult. We just clicked. Perhaps our extroverted natures and independent spirits drew us together, but I could also confide anything without her judging me. During that time, I was a young professional in my thirties, but divorced, broke, and afraid, searching and yearning to gain wisdom about life and love. With me newly single again and Carolyn widowed, we had time for one another, and she became my rock, my sounding board, my guru and my friend.

Carolyn began to fill a void when my immediate family moved out to California during my second year in nursing school, and I made a thoughtful decision to remain in Georgia, which felt like home. When I began working at Children's Healthcare of Atlanta on the Scottish Rite campus, only a few miles from Carolyn's Dunwoody neighborhood, I'd frequently stop by her house after work and take her out to dinner before making the hour-long commute to my home in Lawrenceville. Likewise, I had a standing reservation to spend the night at Carolyn's when I worked late at the hospital and was too tired to make the drive home. Correspondingly, when Carolyn's health issues arose and she required surgery or was hospitalized for a medical ailment, I would stay and care for her at the house in the evenings and sometimes through the night.

Truly a proper lady of the South, complete with Southern drawl and all, Carolyn tossed formalities aside when it came to family and close friends. Since I was considered family, I always entered Carolyn's house through the garage door, certainly not through the front. And while she had a formal living room that was decorated to the nines, I still to this day cannot describe its layout. But the family room, oh, I knew that area by heart. It was the epicenter for all Couch Time with Carolyn sessions.

A long, yellow fabric couch took up most of the wood paneled wall that separated the family and living rooms. Variegated green houseplants covered the fireplace hearth, while numerous sconces and paintings reflected Carolyn's decorating style— where *Southern Living* meets *Better Homes and Gardens*. Bookshelves on either side of the fireplace had amassed all kinds of literary gems, magazines and pictures. Relics from the past (stacks of National Geographic magazines from years gone by; a waist-high, maple antique cabinet displaying a worn, black leather doctor's bag containing medical instruments and a stethoscope, which belonged to Dorothy's grandfather) and the latest technology (a flat screen TV) somehow got along. Carolyn simply had a knack for blending comfort and style. A round coffee table that sat before the couch, for instance, showed off a masterfully arranged silk plant, carefully positioned books and a small bowl of miniature chocolate bars. She had an affinity for chocolate, which I shared.

Carolyn's chair and matching ottoman, both of which were covered in a soft beige fabric that had a hint of yellow to complement the sofa, were command central. Next to her, a tiny decorative maple table held a lamp and a woven basket containing all of Carolyn's must-haves—reading glasses, emery boards, a 1950's-red nail polish and matching matte red lipstick, scissors, pens and pencils. Her phone, paperback romance novels, opened mail, stamps, cards and letters were also kept within arm's reach.

Couch Time sessions began after exchanging of pleasantries, serving Southern-style hors d'oeuvres, such as cheese straws, and pouring a glass of *mother's helper*, Carolyn's code word for chardonnay. We then settled into the family room with wine glasses in hand. I sat on the end of the couch closest to her just like the guest of a late night, talk show host. She positioned herself into her chair, gracefully adjusting her legs onto the ottoman.

We discussed everything—from my work at the hospital, fashion trends and celebrity hook-ups to national, state and local current events. We covered politics, SEC football, cooking, decorating, life, love, marriage and boyfriends. We toasted to life, health and happiness, and sipped our cares away.

I loved hearing Carolyn's stories of growing up in Johnson City, Tennessee, and of her career as a model. She definitely had the physique and beauty. A strikingly tall woman, she possessed delicate features—hazel-blue eyes and alabaster skin, elegantly framed by her short, naturally white curls. In her youth, her hair had been dark brown, which presented a dramatic contrast against her soft complexion in the vintage photos. Reveling in the details of her modeling days and how she met her late husband Preston, Carolyn would pull out her old photographs and newspaper articles, and spread them over the ottoman. One by one, she'd wheeze and draw in deep breaths of air to explain each picture or clipping, reminiscing with fondness in telling stories and describing events.

Of all the photographs she showed me, my favorite was one of her modeling for the local clothier in Johnson City. She stood on the sidewalk next to a shop window, dressed in a gorgeous black, boat-necked dress with dolman sleeves. A narrow black leather belt accentuated her tiny waist and curves, and her long legs were adorned with stylish black pumps that had a dainty bow on the toe of the shoe. A black pleated handbag hung gracefully off her right wrist and her black gloved hands were artfully positioned. A black hat completed the ensemble. Although the photo was black and white, it was evident that Carolyn was wearing her favorite red matte lipstick. (One could also assume that her fingers and toes were painted the same shade, a hue of red that contained blue undertones, which remained a staple in her cosmetics collection throughout her life.) That stunning, statuesque image of her became indelibly etched in my memory.

In the same 1950's fashion, Carolyn would light up a cigarette in preparation for our conversations, which would last well into the evening, and defying current warnings against women smoking, I would join her. I had smoked a little in college, but never learned how to do it properly, or "*prah-per-lee*," as Carolyn would say, so observing her was mesmerizing. She always inhaled the nicotine deeply into her lungs and then slowly blew the smoke into the air, raising her hands for a dramatic effect. I'd roll my blue eyes, laugh and try to mimic her, but as soon as I puffed the smoke into my mouth, I blew it out. I lacked Carolyn's flair with a cigarette, but enjoyed the taste and aroma of the tobacco to complement my glass of wine and piece of chocolate.

Aside from her instructions on the proper way for a lady to handle a cigarette, Couch Time with Carolyn sessions instilled invaluable life lessons over the years: listen to your heart; follow your dreams; open your heart to love. Carolyn actively listened during our conversations. She had the ability to sift through the topic at hand and hit the heart of the matter—*bull's eye*. She, too, enjoyed our time together, all the while knowing that I loved, valued and respected her. I also truly appreciated her confiding in me about her life and struggles with chronic health issues that included the c-word. We were there for each other.

By the time our Couch Time sessions concluded, I possessed a sense of renewal and empowerment. I felt fearless and emerged ready to conquer the world once more.

CHAPTER 4
Invitations

Dorothy had kept the DGs up to speed on Carolyn's condition throughout the month of April, and a visit by Susie and me found her doing quite well. Life continued, and in May, Jeff and I received an "It's a Graduation Party!" invitation for Dorothy's daughter Jennifer. We wouldn't have missed it for the world; I called Robert, Dorothy's second husband, the day it arrived to R.S.V.P. for the event. The party started at two o'clock, and while the afternoon promised to be beautiful with clear skies, the meteorologist on the local morning television station confirmed that temperatures would climb to the mid-80s. Dressed accordingly for the warm weather, Jeff and I climbed into the black Cadillac sedan, air conditioner turned on high, with Jennifer's graduation card and money in hand.

Destination: Lilburn.

During the car ride over to the party, I questioned in my mind how eighteen years could have gone by so fast. Jennifer was graduating from Druid Hills High School. For a period of time, she had chosen to live with her biological dad, Dorothy's first husband, and attend DHHS, which was in his district. Midway through that year, she decided to move back in with Dorothy and Robert, but chose to complete the remainder of her senior year at DHHS. Having worked and earned good grades, she received a scholarship to the University of Tampa and would leave in August to begin her freshman year. Lucky girl, she loved the beach!

With countless lifelong memories of my relationship with Dorothy, my mind sorted through one recollection after another, and I began to reminisce the highlights in chronological order.

Spring, thirty years earlier

I was a freshman at Indiana University in Bloomington, Indiana—and the only Dunwoody High School graduate who went to the Hoosier State for college—when I received a call from Dorothy to tell me about her "big news."

I really wanted to attend the University of Georgia or, better yet, West Georgia College with Dorothy, Carole and Susie. Neither of those schools was in the Big 10 Conference, and I didn't have much of a choice: I.U. was a Hart family tradition. Originally from Indiana, my mother grew up in Indianapolis, and my father was born in a small town about thirty miles east of Indianapolis called Shelbyville. My mother, therefore, went to I.U. My father went to I.U. My uncles and cousins and my dad's cousins also went to I.U. My college destination was predestined by my parents and my ancestors.

Sending me so far away from home, however, my parents made sure I was sequestered in Forest, the all-girls dorm. When Dorothy called, I was sitting in my girls-only room on my girls-only bottom bunk bed. A few months had passed since I'd last seen or spoken with any of the other Dunwoody Girls. The gang had returned home from our respective colleges for winter break to celebrate the holidays. Then tragedy struck. Susie's mom Dolly suddenly passed away from a massive heart attack one day before New Year's Eve. She battled diabetes all of her life, and the disease became too much for her heart and body to handle any longer. Dolly was the first of the DG parents to die. It was a somber time; we were eighteen years old.

Thinking of Susie, I interrupted Dorothy's announcement to ask, "So, how's Sus' doing?" I knew she had returned to college after the family funeral in Connecticut.

"She's hangin' in there," Dorothy offered. "Some days are better than others." Moving on, she asked, "Hey, what are you doing this summer? I have plans for you."

"Okay," I said. "Where are we going?" At that point, I was thinking the big news was about us all going on some exotic beach trip to Florida. I'd had enough of the bone chilling cold, snow, slush and ice, and couldn't wait to trade in my full-length down coat (it made me look like the Michelin Man) for a bathing suit.

"I'm getting married!" Dorothy blurted out.

Fantasies of the Florida trip evaporated like snow under the hot Georgia sun. My thoughts went from *where are we going* to *what are you doing?*

"What?" I stammered into the phone receiver. "To whom?"

Over Christmas break, Dorothy had said she was dating a guy at the University of Georgia, but I had no idea how serious their relationship had gotten. *Wow! Married!* Dorothy had turned nineteen years old just two months earlier.

"I want you to be in the wedding—you, Carole, Susan, and Susie," she continued. "My sister Margaret is going to be my maid of honor." Reassuring me that she was completely sane and not pregnant, Dorothy went on to unveil her nuptial plans scheduled for that summer.

I was in awe. Dorothy had found her true love, and so quickly. The rest of the DGs were still very single, searching for Mr. Right, or settling for Mr. Alright, or dumping Mr. Not Right. The news took some time to sink in. *Dorothy was getting married*. She was going to be a Mrs. I was giddy, mostly from the invitation and idea of being part of a wedding party and having the opportunity to own my first poufy bridesmaid dress and dye-matched satin shoes.

Gosh! We were so naïve back then, I thought.

My memory shifted to Dorothy's wedding and then to my mine—the first, failed one. What I once believed was an ideal marriage had dissolved with the tap of a judge's gavel.

Recalling the end of that relationship, I saw myself back on Carolyn's couch soon after that divorce—the first Couch Time with Carolyn session.

CHAPTER 5

Couch Time with Carolyn Lesson #1:
Listen to Your Heart

I sipped my glass of chardonnay, tucked my bare feet underneath me on the couch and settled in for our Couch Time session. Carolyn lit up a cigarette. She took in a deep drag and pursed her red lips, blowing the swirls of smoke high above her head. Subconsciously, her left hand waved away the haze and cleared the air between us. She leaned in. Our eyes locked.

"Why do you think your first marriage wasn't successful?" she asked, making the most of her opportunity to pose some probing questions. "I know you loved him and you seemed to be happy on the outside, but what really happened? Lord knows you had such a beautiful wedding at Dunwoody United Methodist Church. Preston and I were totally blown away by the event, the fleet of white limos and Lincoln Town Cars, and even the tour buses to take us downtown to the Sloppy Floyd Building for the reception." Carolyn leaned back in her chair and raised her outstretched legs onto the ottoman; she was obviously settling in for the long story answer.

I was saying *dammit* to myself while also hearing my sister Julie's voice telling me to substitute *sugar snaps* for the profanity. *Well, dammit and sugar snaps!*

There would be no dodging the topic of divorce that night, and for a moment, I felt like I might as well have been sitting on the couch naked. The vulnerable sensation led me to recall skinny-dipping as a kid for the first time in a cold Indiana lake at night. I was at summer camp. The risky behavior was the scariest and most liberating thing I'd experienced up to that point in my life. Nevertheless, I felt safe and knew I wasn't going to get into trouble because my older cousin Ann was my camp counselor. Another comfort was having my cousin Emily, the same age as I, swimming alongside of me in her birthday suit.

Noting a similar sense of feeling exposed and not knowing what would surface, I acknowledged that I was in a safe place on Carolyn's couch. I could hear the voices of my cousins encouraging me, *Katie, just jump in the water with both feet*. Pushing me, they said in my head, *You need to talk about it. You need to open up.* I took a sip of wine and then cradled the glass between my hands. *You need to break down the barriers*. Hints of pear and oak warmed my palate. *You need to figure out why it failed so it doesn't happen again*. Stalling, I released my left hand from the glass and slowly raked my fingers through my long hair. *Don't be afraid.*

To end my cousins' imagined appeals and get on with Carolyn's in-person inquiry, I breathed deeply, peeled back my exoskeleton, and uttered, "Gosh, where do I begin?" Tapping into my inner smartass to keep me sane through the pain, I said, "There were so many red flags from the get-go that it looked like we were plotting a red out at a Georgia Bulldog football game. And yet, I was completely blind to them all."

"Oh, sweetie," Carolyn responded, wheezing out a laugh. "Just start from the beginning," she added after a coughing spell. "I want to hear all about it."

"I was young, in my early twenties," I said. "If you remember, I was accepted into Georgia State University's School of Nursing, so instead of staying in The Hoosier State for two more years, I was happily preparing to move back home after my sophomore year to thaw out, a process that began with spring break. Dorothy was already married, but the other DGs had planned an excursion to Panama City Beach, Florida. We were in a Pizza Hut one night during that trip when we ran into a group of boys from Ohio. Steve and his friends were also on vacation, so our two groups merged and we partied the weekend away. That's when our worlds collided.

"Steve and I clicked," I acknowledged. "But knowing he was hundreds of miles away attending Notre Dame University, I didn't give *us* another thought."

"He thought differently?" Carolyn asked.

"Yes," I said, thinking back. "Yes, he did. I never gave him my phone number. However, he was resourceful, calling and convincing Georgia State to give him my contact information. And he was persistent. In the months that followed, he phoned; he wrote letters; he mailed cards; he even sent flowers.

"Our two groups coordinated another spring break vacation in Florida the next year, so we got together again during that trip. Steve would then move to Atlanta after graduation for a hotel management job. Of course, he later switched careers, entering the sports marketing field and the world of NASCAR and racing. Underneath it all, his big life dream was to discover and manage a big, popular musical group.

"After graduating, we both proceeded with what we perceived was the proper order of life events, or what family and friends expected of us and we of ourselves. I settled into my nursing career at the children's hospital, and Steve and I entered a serious relationship.

"Shortly after his relocation, on Groundhog Day, we were engaged. He didn't ask my dad for my hand in marriage, dismissive of the tradition."

Carolyn frowned and made a mental note.

"We married on February 20, one year after Steve proposed."

"Ah, such a beautiful day!" Carolyn said, using her hands for emphasis. "Such a beautiful wedding." While she repeated the words, ashes flew through the air.

"Ah," I countered, wagging my right index finger at her, "but little did you know all that went on behind the scenes leading up to our wedding and during the day of the affair."

"Ooooh, do tell me all the juicy details, sweetie!" She exclaimed. "And don't leave out a thing."

"For starters," I said, "the wedding had some bad luck elements, especially concerning our grandmothers. Over the weeks leading up to the big day, Steve's Grandma Rose got very sick and was hospitalized, so she wasn't able to attend. Ironically, Gigi, my grandma, almost ended up in the hospital, too."

Carolyn's wide eyes and open mouth showed that the information shocked her.

"It happened at an extended stay hotel. Dad had booked an entire wing of rooms at a place off Roswell Road so that out-of-town guests and others of us could be together for the events. In the middle of the night prior to the rehearsal dinner, Gigi got up to use the bathroom. Confused in the darkness about where she was, she fell and broke her arm. Unbelievably, she didn't cry out or wake us to tell us that she had hurt herself until the next morning."

"Oh my goodness!" Carolyn said, shuddering. "She had to have been in so much pain. Now remind me: She's your mom's mom?"

"I know, right?" I said, wincing in reference to my grandma's painful ordeal. "And, yes, Gigi was Mom's mom. We learned that she made a cocktail and downed some pain pills, then propped her arm up with pillows and waited until dawn. When we found her, she was sitting up in bed wearing her crystal encrusted, silver framed glasses. Being a nurse, she'd made herself a makeshift sling, and on top of that, she was already dressed for the day. She had even somehow managed to fashion her white hair into a bun. Of course, as soon as she told us what happened, Dad scooped up Gigi and put her in the car. I drove her to Northside Hospital's emergency room and stayed until the orthopedic doctors released her. After everything, despite feeling completely worn out and drugged out, Gigi insisted she'd attend the rehearsal dinner. And she did!"

"Gigi was such a trooper—a total spitfire!" Carolyn confirmed, placing her right hand over her heart as if she were about to recite The Pledge of Allegiance. "A woman after my own heart," she added.

"Wasn't she though?" I agreed. "She bought a special outfit for the dinner, and come hell or high water, nothing was going to stop her from going. Not even a broken arm."

Carolyn and I toasted to Gigi with a proper click of our glasses followed by a sip of the wine. Setting our glasses down without sipping first would have been bad form and, we believed, bad luck!

"Well," Carolyn commented, "I had no idea you had two grandmas down for the count before the wedding."

"Oh, wait," I injected, "there's more. I'm just getting warmed up."

Rising from her chair, Carolyn raised her hands, signaling me to refrain from uttering another word until she retrieved another bottle of wine from the kitchen. Opening a second bottle was unusual. Traditionally, sessions required up to two glasses of wine apiece, but this Couch Time with Carolyn session urged her to pour a third glass for certain and possibly a forth.

I had to agree with her. *Heck just set the bottle down in front of me*, I thought. My nerves were completely shot from dredging up the memories. *How did I get so lost? Will I ever find true love? Only forty dollars remain in my bank account and I no longer have a savings account. What am I going to do to make ends meet? How can I make more money? Who am I supposed to be? Where am I going? I want to throw up.*

Carolyn returned, and after topping off our glasses, she settled back into her chair and waved her hand to carry on. I took a sip to quell my current worries and think back to where it all went wrong.

"The day of the wedding was totally crazy," I said after a moment. "Following the nuptials, the limos, the Town Cars, and the busses caravanned to downtown Atlanta where the festivities began. Music played, drinks flowed and dinner commenced as planned. But when the time came for the traditional father-daughter dance, I couldn't find my dad anywhere. As soon as I sent out a search party for him, Mom came running up to me with her strand of pearls swinging from her chest. She was nearly breathless."

In the best Mom voice I could muster, I imitated how she sounded. "Your father … is … in the coat closet … with your Aunt Pat … and your cousin Emily. Now … don't … you … worry. The ambulance … and … the paramedics … are on their way. The … serving staff … has your Aunt Pat … breathing … into … a paper bag … now … that she has regained … consciousness."

"What the heck?" Carolyn blurted, sitting upright in her chair.

"I was standing in the middle of the dance floor with an image of Aunt Pat lying on the floor amongst the racks of coats, breathing into a brown paper bag with my Dad, serving staff and Emily—in her pink, poufy, taffeta bridesmaid dress—by her side," I said. "The idea of it all made my head spin, but I remembered telling Mom I needed to shed my veil and get a stethoscope to help. Mom, however, insisted that I stay put. There were plenty of people in the coatroom assisting, she'd said, and, in fact, the paramedics and the stretcher had arrived.

"Mom then told Steve and me to carry on as if nothing was wrong as she and her pearl necklace bolted out of the room." I looked at Carolyn, who was shaking her head in disbelief. "Steve responded by rejoining his friends. Abandoned on the dance floor, I just stood there observing a sea of people who were totally oblivious to the drama going on down the hall. At last, my eyes rested on Gigi. Dressed up in a new suit and wearing a broach on her sling, she was swigging a highball and carrying on with one of the groomsmen.

"What am I going to do? Will Aunt Pat be alright? Who am I going to dance with? Submerged by the flood of questions without answers, I was all but paralyzed on that parquet floor. Fortunately, my Uncle Bill got wind of the ordeal and immediately ran over to rescue me. With impeccable timing, he scooped me into his arms as the DJ began playing 'Daddy's Little Girl.'

"The ambulance took Aunt Pat to Georgia Baptist Hospital," I informed Carolyn. "Dad and Emily left the party to be with her. Come to find out," I added, "Aunt Pat had an underlying heart problem that she was totally unaware of ... until the day of our wedding."

Satisfied with the explanation, Carolyn sat back in her chair. "So that explains why Preston and I never saw your parents at the reception."

"Yup ... and there's more," I continued. "Steve and I returned to the extended stay hotel with his parents, and they asked us to join his family in their suite before we were driven to an airport hotel for the night because we had to catch a flight to Cancun early the next morning. Well, we had our suitcases in hand when his parents decided to tell us that they were flying out to New York the following day. Remember, Carolyn, they lived in Ohio.

Come to find out, Grandma Rose had passed away a few days prior to the wedding. The family was going to New York to attend her funeral."

Carolyn perched on the edge of her seat, grasping the arms of the chair. "Oh … my … goodness, sweetie. His grandma passed away before the wedding and they didn't tell you until afterwards?"

"They were being so sweet," I explained, "and just thought it was best to withhold the information until we were ready to hear it. They insisted we continue on to Mexico, despite our objections to change our flight plans. It's a good thing that Andy, Steve's best man, drove us to the other hotel; Steve and I were crying in the backseat all the way there."

"How romantic!" Carolyn exclaimed. "What a way to start out a marriage." Loosening her grip on the chair, she eased back into a comfortable position.

Exhausted from reliving the rollercoaster wedding fiasco, Carolyn and I sipped from our glasses of chardonnay. She also fired up a cigarette and so did I. The act of drawing smoke into my mouth, letting the taste of the tobacco dance on my tongue, and immediately blowing it out into the den calmed the calamity and numbed my feelings.

"I thought I was ready," I told Carolyn and myself. "I was in love. However, within five short years after we said, 'I do,' I figured out that Steve wasn't the man I thought he was, wished that he was, or hoped that he could be for me."

Memories invaded my mind. "We were one year into our marriage and had purchased our first house in Lawrenceville," I reminded Carolyn. "Steve was employed as the Director of Marketing for Road Atlanta," I said, referring to a well-known automotive race course about fifty miles north of the city in Hall County. "In contrast, I worked fifteen minutes from home as a nurse at Egleston Pediatric Hospital's urgent care center. While living our lives together under one roof, we were on two different life tracks, pursuing our dreams separately.

"Steve also had a short temper," I went on. "He was at ease berating people. With each incident, a little piece of me withered inside. It wasn't his fault. He was who he was, and looking back through the life events we shared together, I knew in my heart that I wasn't the right person for him; I realized he didn't have the qualities that I needed in a husband."

Carolyn raised her eyebrows, as if prompting me to elaborate.

"You know this story," I said, "but not the specifics. During one of our many Road Atlanta weekend events at the track, I was approached by a publisher from *Atlanta Women's News* magazine to participate in the All Women's Road Rally. The magazine wanted to know if I could drive the Road Atlanta pace car. The owners of the track thought it was a great idea and quickly gave their blessing, but Steve was not convinced and certainly not thrilled. He thought I might embarrass him or the track, possibly wreck the car, or all of the above. I was hurt that he didn't believe in me and felt another piece of me wither away.

"Deep down, however, I knew who I was and what I was made of. *Give me the keys, move over and let me drive. I'll show you what I can do,* I remember thinking.

"The Road Rally was a timed event on a predetermined course," I explained, in case Carolyn didn't remember the details. "Drivers were routed through North Georgia with checkpoints to cross at specific times throughout the day. The rules were simple. Each team had two women—a driver and a navigator. They would receive instructions at each checkpoint that specified directions and speeds for reaching the next checkpoint.

"What made the race interesting were the uncontrollable factors from driving through the small towns—traffic lights, other cars, railroad crossings—and even the possibility of car trouble. Any or all of those elements would impact a team's time, but none of the participants were told how much time they were officially allotted, which was based upon the race officials' predetermined calculations. Therefore, the race involved following the rules as well as a strategy. Minutes were deducted from the total score if the car crossed the checkpoint early or added if the car got lost and crossed late. The team closest to the ideal score won the race.

"I had a great strategy from the start. I decided I would drive the car and choose one of the other DGs to be the navigator. When I thought about who could remain calm under pressure, follow instructions and give clear directions, one DG name rose to the top of the list: Carole."

Carolyn looked a bit disappointed that I hadn't chosen Dorothy, so I said, "If you'll recall, Carole was single at the time. Dorothy's weekends were busy with married life and attending the home Georgia Bulldog games. So, Carole quickly jumped at the invitation. Neither of us could wait for the big day. Nothing, not even Steve's grumbling objections on the morning of the race could spoil my excitement. Seeing our yellow Nissan 300ZX pace car—with big, blue block letters spelling 'Road Atlanta' on the hood and red and blue racing stripes swirling across the doors—made it easy for me to remain consciously oblivious to him. Much to the chagrin of Steve, Carole and I eagerly hopped into the car, buckled in for the daylong race, and disappeared down the kudzu-lined back roads of North Georgia.

"When the race concluded that evening, I dropped Carole off at her apartment and drove myself home. Steve's parents were in town, so I found Steve and his dad standing at the foot of the fireplace in the den, deeply engaged in conversation. Without a word, I walked between them and placed a gold and blue trophy, crowned with a gold car, on the fireplace mantle. The plaque at the base of the award read '2nd Place, Atlanta Women's News, 1989 All Women's Road Rally.' Without skipping a beat, I turned and exited. Calling from the kitchen, I said, 'Dinner will be ready in thirty minutes.'"

Carolyn smiled, amused, but didn't comment so I could finish.

"The second-place prize package for each of us included a set of four racing tires, an autographed book by female IndyCar racing legend Lyn St. James, tickets to an upcoming event in Atlanta featuring Oprah and renowned hairstylist José Eber, a free haircut at a local salon, and a trophy. I know that you remember when we appeared on the front cover of *Atlanta Women's News* magazine," I added.

"Carole and I had hooted and hollered all the way home from the race, thrilled beyond our wildest dreams that we even placed in the event," I went on. "Leaving behind all of our fears and inhibitions in the dust behind us, we had driven our hearts out that day. But my first husband didn't have the heart to appreciate that kind of accomplishment or share my joy."

Pausing, I waved away the smoke from my cigarette and crushed the butt into the ashtray. Just like that, I snuffed out the memory as well.

"The little things added up to my decision to get a divorce from Steve," I told Carolyn. "Even so, I was really scared about going it alone and deeply concerned about what my parents would think and what Steve's family would think. His family was very good to me, and I really loved them all. I was afraid of disappointing them, but I had fallen out of love with Steve. Unbeknownst to me, however, my feelings had become apparent to my parents."

"How did you tell your mom and dad?" Carolyn asked, about to light her fourth cigarette.

"Our fifth anniversary was approaching," I responded, "and the closer the day came, the more adamant and confident I became about my decision. Over the previous year, I had suggested that we try counseling to help improve our relationship and communication. Steve rejected the idea. Another piece of me shriveled, so I sought out a therapist— alone. After sorting through my thoughts and feelings, I knew what I needed to do; I was emotionally detached from our relationship.

"When I finally mustered enough courage to call my parents with my decision and heard their reactions, I was shocked, especially by Dad's response. 'Watching you in this marriage is like watching a flower die on the vine,' he informed me. 'Your mother and I love you too much to see this happen to you. You are such a joyous person and have so much to offer someone. Your mother and I totally support you in this decision and we're always here for you.' Mom couldn't resist the urge to weigh in and chimed, 'You know, Gigi predicted you wouldn't stay with him.'

"I recall thinking, *Really? Even Gigi knew that I wasn't happy? Was it that obvious? Was I that oblivious to my own feelings? My God!*

"I immediately started crying," I told Carolyn. "Tears flowed because I was overwhelmed by my parent's support and love. Overwhelmed by my dad's comments. Overwhelmed and relieved that I wasn't going to be going through this divorce alone. Overwhelmed by grief for the loss of this marriage. Overwhelmed that it was so apparently obvious to everyone, including Gigi, but not me, until the moment I confessed to my parents. I was overwhelmed by what I had hoped for, wished for and prayed that it could be, but it wasn't. Overwhelmed because I needed to start my life over from scratch.

"Through the tears, I remember asking my parents, 'If it was becoming so clear to you all that I wasn't happy, why didn't you say anything to me?' They told me that I wouldn't have listened to them. I really needed to figure it out on my own and in my own time."

"So true, sweetie," Carolyn offered, nodding her head in agreement with my parents' response. "So true. They were absolutely right about that. You wouldn't have listened to them at all. You would become defensive, and it would have caused a great rift between your parents, Steve and his family." As if to put a period at the end of her comment, she tapped the end of her cigarette with her right index finger, and the ashes fell into the ceramic bowl below.

"Dad and I had never had such an intimate discussion before," I said. "*Never.* His words struck me like arrows through my heart, and they were all I needed to hear. I knew who I was and what I was made of. I just needed a husband who truly respected me and appreciated who I was and the love I had to give."

"Sometimes life tests you," Carolyn said. "You don't get a study guide or a warning that it's coming. You have to be able to stand on your own. It's pass or fail. Ultimately, the choices you make determine the direction you will go. I know it wasn't an easy decision for you, and you didn't make that choice lightly. I can tell that it weighed heavily on your heart. However, you grew so much more confident from your life experiences. They made you stronger. You learned what you would and wouldn't tolerate. You learned that there is a difference between loving someone and being in love with someone. Those experiences defined you." She snuffed out her cigarette and concluded, "And you chose to bravely listen to your heart."

The past coupled with Carolyn's compassion elicited a stream of tears, and I wiped them away from my cheeks. "I can remember the day Steve met me at the attorney's office to sign the quick claim deed to the house," I said, staring into my glass as I swirled the amber liquid. "As we walked out to our cars, he informed me that he had no idea that I was capable of seeing the divorce through and didn't know how I had figured out all of the necessary steps to see it to completion."

"My gosh!" Carolyn said. "What did you say to that?"

"I told him that was because he had no idea who he had married," I said to Carolyn. "With that, I got into my car and drove away, uncertain and scared. I didn't know where life was going to take me. I left him standing next to his car with his shrinking image in my rear view mirror. As excruciatingly painful as it was, I knew in that moment I had made the right decision — for me.

"At that time," I persisted, "his barb did not penetrate my skin. I did not let it. Not one piece of me withered away; instead, I actually bloomed and grew. Through the separation and divorce process, I became introspective, listening to my heart, soul and mind. I prayed and kept a journal. I even read numerous inspirational books and in the process came across a quote from Maya Angelou that I adopted as one of my favorites: 'The first time someone shows you who they are, believe them.'"

Allowing various segments of my life to pass before my eyes, I must have gazed down momentarily. When I looked up, Carolyn winked and smiled. "Sweetie," she said, "you have the opportunity to set out into this world and be the young lady you always dreamed of becoming. What do you want to do with your life? Your career? What kind of guy would be your ideal husband? These are all things you need to think about, etch and sort out. Life has given you a second chance, a clean slate. Now forge your own story. Don't be afraid. You need to let go of the past and move forward."

She paused and added, "By the way, you passed."

CHAPTER 6

A New Life Begins

My mind was taking me on quite a journey while Jeff drove us across town to Jennifer's graduation party. Realizing we still had halfway to go until we reached Dorothy's house, I let myself return to the past.

Once again, I thought about the high marks Carolyn had given me for wisely ending my marriage. In truth, walking away had been relatively easy once I'd made up my mind; the real test came after, especially in the immediate months after the divorce. I struggled financially on my single paycheck, but I was determined to figure out the solutions myself and learn to become self-sufficient.

Right away, I met with the bank to refinance loans into affordable monthly payments that allowed me to keep my car and house. I also found a roommate to help curtail the household expenses. Focusing also on my professional career, I took on multiple jobs to make ends meet. I didn't want to downsize, sell the house or ask my parents for money, and I had chosen not to ask for alimony. I never wanted to be financially dependent on Steve. I had severed the ties emotionally and financially so I could be free to proceed with my life on my own.

One of the first steps I took towards achieving financial freedom was in becoming a certified aerobics instructor. I taught countless classes at the former Falcon Sports and Fitness Complex, a popular sporting and racquetball club in Suwanee, Georgia, located next to the Atlanta Falcon's original training camp and offices. That job led to another opportunity; the Atlanta Falcons contracted me to work as a team nurse for a summer.

I worked hard but also I realized that I loved the administrative and strategic planning side of the healthcare industry. In turn, I was quickly promoted and then hired by The Emory Clinic pediatric orthopedic group that worked at Egleston Children's Hospital as their nurse manager. I was twenty-nine years old.

I was in the midst of setting my sights and feet in forward motion when Dorothy called to tell me she was pregnant. The first DG to get married, she would also be the first to have a baby. *Wow! A baby!* I couldn't believe she was going to be a mom, but her news wasn't all I needed to digest: Dorothy had a favor to ask of me.

"Shoot," I encouraged her. "Ask away—as long as it's legal," I joked.

"Would you mind coming with me to my Lamaze classes?" Her tone was apologetic. "My husband isn't interested in going, and well … uh … the whole birthing thing kind of grosses him out."

Recalling the graphic birthing videos we had to watch in nursing school that prepared and educated us for the labor and delivery section of our training, I laughed out loud. On one hand, I couldn't really blame the man: blood, secretions, pee, poop, bottoms and vaginas. Yup, you pretty much got to see it all and it definitely wasn't for the faint of heart. On the other hand,

Dorothy and I both knew the real reason why her husband wasn't interested, but we didn't mention the truth.

I agreed to become Dorothy's Lamaze partner. I would have done anything for her, been anywhere she needed me to be at any given moment in the world. The DGs were all at each other's beck and call. Therefore, just like an eager student on the first day of class, I inquired about her expectations of my duties and clarified the list of supplies that I would need in order to be proactively involved.

Dorothy's Lamaze classes were being held in a medical office building near three major hospitals: Scottish Rite Children's Hospital, Northside Hospital and St. Joe's—an area long ago coined "Pill Hill" for its geographic convergence of the hospitals and related medical complexes. From my professional work and training, I was quite familiar with that part of town.

On the night of our first Lamaze class, a few weeks after the pregnancy announcement call, I left work and drove over to Pill Hill. Casually noting the customary furniture and well-manicured green plants filling the lobby, I took the elevator up to meet Dorothy. She was waiting in the hallway so we could walk in the class together.

"Here, this is for you," Dorothy said, handing me a pillow from a guest bed in her home. I smiled to myself imagining how she had chosen the freshly washed, floral scented, flowered pillowcase to make a positive first impression. As soon as we entered the classroom through a big wooden door, however, I felt uncomfortable, to say the least.

A Lamaze class provided couples the opportunity to bond more closely, delving into a new layer of intimacy, before they became Mom and Dad. In contrast, I was single and dating, still searching for true love, while Dorothy, who would soon bring a child into the world, was anticipating the joyful experience of a mother's love yet coping with a troubled marriage. The reality that her ideal marriage was dissolving had me scared for her and the new baby.

I knew the only thing that really mattered was our choice to be there for each other in times of need, and I clutched the newly acquired pillow tightly to my chest like a life preserver. I clung to it for dear life.

Sink or swim, just jump in with both feet. Here we go.

Determined to be there for Dorothy, I scanned the classroom. A television, a video tape player, plastic pelvises with pretend babies, and anatomical flipcharts were scattered around the periphery. Expectant moms and dads occupied most of the plastic chairs, which were arranged in a circle. Dorothy and I did not want to be conspicuous; however, we were not only among the last to arrive, but also a female couple.

Oh, thank God, we're not alone, I thought, sighing with relief, when I took notice of one other female pairing.

Nevertheless, through each introduction, Dorothy stressed emphatically that we were best friends and she was married. Pointing to the ring on her left hand, she found some way to say that her husband either didn't want to or couldn't attend the training sessions. Likewise, I can't be sure if I said or just thought what was on my mind: *He is a butthead for not being here for her.*

Being there for Dorothy certainly allowed us to share a variety of experiences together. We watched a lot of educational and informative birthing videos involving natural births, births in the hospital, C-section births, births at home, and even births in and under water. I didn't think I would ever look at a tub or a kiddie pool the same way again. Thankfully, the beautiful birthing experiences all ended with tearfully joyful parents, kissing their brand new baby while expressing their enduring love for each other and for their child.

From witnessing many births during my nurses training, I definitely viewed the birthing process as a miraculous event and babies as the ultimate miracles, but Dorothy and I were not above cutting up like school kids in a sex education class. We shared in the best of times through the *he-he-he* and *ho-ho-ho* breathing pattern exercises with me squashing Dorothy into an upright sitting position while she pretended to expel the baby. Frequently, especially during intimate and awkward moments, giggling fits seized us, and my pillow became useful for burying my face to suppress bouts of laughter.

I thought Dorothy and I would never regain our composure the first time she had to practice the breathing-pushing technique by wiggling in backwards between my open, outstretched legs and leaning up against me. We just had to stop looking at each other. Otherwise, if we caught each other's eyes, the giggling fits would return until tears ran down our cheeks. My whispered serenades into Dorothy's ear of "Having my Baby," the old classic crooned by Paul Anka, and "Can't Get Enough of Your Love Baby" by the legendary baby-making singer, Barry White, were the ultimate tools for breaking down any uncomfortable barriers between us.

Through it all, we made our best attempts to keep ourselves focused and restrained, although we often had to force ourselves to remain professional and take the training seriously. I will never forget, as long as I live, the first or the last day of those Lamaze coaching classes. I'm sure the instructor and the other expectant parents in our class won't either.

Despite all of our preparation, the call I received after midnight from Dorothy's husband turned out not to be a notice to meet her at Northside Hospital for the birthing process. Instead, Dorothy, having gone into labor earlier, had already given birth to a baby girl, Jennifer Rose. Both mother and daughter were doing fine.

Along with good news, his stressful tone indicated a cause for concern, and he said the birth had some complications and ended in a C-section. I would later learn from Dorothy that "some complications" ended up being seizures (called eclampsia), high blood pressure and fetal distress. Thanks to an emergency C-section, Dorothy and Jennifer were lucky to be alive.

Since Dorothy's husband returned to work right away, Carolyn remained at Dorothy's bedside during her recuperation in the hospital, and I periodically checked in on them on my way home from the hospital. On one of my afternoon visits, I learned that mom and baby were doing well, but Dorothy couldn't wait to wash the "hospital funk" off her body. While Carolyn flipped through her *Southern Living* magazine, Dorothy lifted the white net band around her belly to show me the staples securing her abdominal incision. She went on to say that she had been waiting for a nurse to help give her a shower.

"How long have you been waiting?" I inquired, pulling up a chair to sit beside her.

"All day," Dorothy replied.

"Wha-a-a-at? No-o-o-o!" I exclaimed, popping up from my chair. "Are you kidding me?" I kicked off my high-heeled shoes and Carolyn read my mind. Nodding her head in the affirmative, she rose to her feet and placed the magazine on her chair.

Together, we helped Dorothy get out of the bed, and in no time, Carolyn, Dorothy, the beeping, blue IV pump on the rolling pole and I were crammed into the tiny hospital bathroom. Dorothy was weak, shaky and unsteady from the trauma of the delivery—it was a miracle that neither she nor the baby died or suffered major side effects from the ordeal—so I stepped into the shower with her. Still wearing a business suit, I really didn't care if it got a little wet as I steadied her under the shower head. Carolyn, meanwhile, stood beside the stall with the IV pole. Her job was to hold the IV tubing so it would not catch on anything and potentially rip out of Dorothy's hand.

Operation Shower Show succeeded: Dorothy felt cleaner than ever, and we dried her, re-dressed her in a clean hospital gown, and returned her safely to the bed.

When Dorothy's evening nurse appeared, she caught me toweling myself dry and gave me a look that implied, *What the heck are you doing wet?* Dismissing me with a scoff, she turned her attention to Dorothy's IV bag and asked if she needed anything.

"Nope," Dorothy said with a smile, "not anymore!"

We all had a good laugh—of course, after the nurse exited the room. I could only imagine if she had walked in on the three of us. The only perfectly reasonable response would have been for us to have smiled back at her from the shower stall and shouted, *Surprise!*—complete with jazz hands, of course!

CHAPTER 7

The Graduation Party

Jeff parked the car in front of Dorothy and Robert's house. The vivid memories, a mental reel featuring highlights from my past with Dorothy, quickly dissolved and faded to black as their colonial style, red brick house, complete with black shutters and white trim, materialized. We had arrived for Jennifer's graduation party and so had numerous other guests. Cars lined the curbs on both sides of the street. I knew that Dorothy expected a big group, including friends from the neighborhood and church.

A gardenia bush in full bloom welcomed us with a heavenly aroma as we approached via the concrete walkway, and Jennifer greeted us in the foyer with squeals of delight. We exchanged hugs and kisses, and then left her to receive other guests and graciously accept their cards and gifts. Jeff and I weaved our way through the buzzing crowd into the noisy kitchen, where one of the guests was pulling a tray of Chick-fil-A chicken nuggets from the oven. *Another yummy aroma!* We spotted Dorothy and Robert, but they were busy making introductions and taking drink orders, so Jeff and I went from room to room, surveying the party.

Red tablecloths, graduation confetti, fresh flower bouquets, and plenty to eat and drink—finger and snack foods, vegetable and fruit trays, a huge graduation chocolate chip cookie cake, red punch and more—had been painstakingly prepared and now enjoyed by a parade of people. The sweet smell of icing and chocolate from Jennifer's cake lured Jeff and me in for a closer look, and that's when Dorothy joined us.

After telling us how much Jennifer loved chocolate chip cookie cakes, Dorothy unexpectedly grabbed my hand and ushered me through the bustling crowds in the dining room and kitchen. We settled on the temporarily unoccupied screened-in porch. The room, with its usual white wicker furniture and floral cushions, had a table stocked with various sodas and water bottles, serving as a beverage station for the day's festivities.

"Are you okay?" I asked, searching her face for answers.

"No," she said hastily. "Mom couldn't come to the party today. She isn't doing very well at all. She had to be admitted to St. Joe's on Friday night." I was shocked to learn that Carolyn had been in the hospital for almost two days.

"Mom hasn't eaten anything solid for the past three weeks," Dorothy said, "and she's having a hard time keeping anything down. She's been battling nausea for almost a month now. Mom's liver and her kidney functions are failing, too. Her belly is swelling with fluid as a result. Doctors drained off the excess fluid collecting in her abdomen on Friday, but it rapidly returned."

Tears welled in my eyes and spilled down my face.

"The doctors give Mom about three more weeks," Dorothy added. Her eyes, also filling with tears, darted away from mine and stared off into the distance.

Her words struck me like a gunshot to my heart. *Three weeks—to live, to die.*

I felt my knees go weak.

"Does Jennifer know?" I asked, wiping tears from my chin with the back of my hand.

"No, I haven't told her all of the details." She added, "I didn't want to distract her from her graduation party."

Two months had gone by since Dorothy first called to relay the doctor's prognosis of Carolyn's condition. We weren't expecting to see such drastic changes so soon, but the tide had evidently turned. Her remaining months with us were now reduced to days.

I looked at Dorothy and squeezed her hand. "How are you holding up?"

"Not very well," she admitted. "I've been crying off and on all weekend long. I've notified work. I have completed my FMLA paperwork, so I plan on being with her until the end. Margaret isn't planning on coming home from Texas until Brad graduates from high school on June 2—unless, of course, Mom passes away before then." Dorothy whispered, "I'm not sure if Mom can hang on that long."

Based on Carolyn's new signs and symptoms, I had to agree with her—in silence. A look of worry veiled her face as she ran her hands through her thick, brown hair. Before I had time to console her, guests emerged on the porch to get drinks, and Dorothy, quickly changing the subject, was commenting on how she had missed her hair appointment that morning and badly needed a cut and color.

We attended to the guests and exchanged pleasantries, and inquired about their upcoming Memorial Day plans over the weekend. While they filled their plastic cups with ice and soda, Dorothy pointed out that there was plenty of food to eat in the dining room. Thankfully, they responded by making a beeline towards the buffet table and left us alone.

Dorothy knew that Carolyn was like a second mother to me, and the suddenness of it hit us both hard—really hard. Having to say it out loud made it real—really real. We hugged each other and started to cry again, uncontrollably. Dorothy would soon experience another first among the DGs as the first to lose both parents.

Immediately, Dorothy and I had to process the facts and adapt to the unexpected turn of events facing Carolyn. With the enduring love and support of her family and from the DGs, we would persevere and survive the ordeal together with style and grace. Deciding on the time that I would visit Carolyn in the hospital the next day, we quickly dried our tears, recomposed ourselves and refocused our attention back to reason for the day's celebration: Jennifer.

CHAPTER 8

Couch Time with Carolyn Lesson #2:
Follow Your Dreams

I helped Carolyn into her chair and poured her a glass of wine. We had just finished eating dinner in the kitchen, an Italian meal to-go from a chain restaurant located around the corner. After working a long day at the hospital, I cherished Carolyn's invitations to join her for dinner and Couch Time. Leaning over the coffee table, I sorted through the mini chocolate bars in the bowl and decided upon a Krackel—dessert! I peeled back the red wrapper and popped the treat into my mouth. Settling back against the yellow couch, I comfortably crossed my legs and savored the melting chocolate and crispy rice.

On that night, like many others, I had packed an overnight bag knowing I'd have to get up early the next morning for a six-thirty meeting with a physician. In my mid-thirties and still unmarried, I dated now and again but remained more focused on my professional career. To supplement my income, I had begun writing, first for medical journals, then for professional publications. Busy honing my craft and becoming an expert in the field of pediatric orthopedics and sports medicine, I joined the Orthopaedic Nurses Association and got highly involved in the Atlanta Chapter. From the affiliation, I met an amazingly talented group of men and women who practiced at various hospitals and clinics throughout Atlanta and surrounding areas. I also traveled the country, lecturing on a broad spectrum of pediatric orthopedic and healthcare topics, and loved opening myself up to new opportunities.

While my work schedule (being on call 24/7 and having office hours bookended with early morning and late night meetings) proved to be taxing, I managed to carve out time for a controlled social life. Baynham, a.k.a. Susan on the rare occasion that any DG called her by her first name, was also single at the time, and she played a big role in stimulating my personal calendar. She encouraged me to join a sports and fitness social group, and we spent our weekends together playing an assortment of recreational sports, from softball and flag football to tennis. We also descended upon Atlanta's social scene, frequenting many bars and restaurants in Buckhead and other metro hotspots. Occasionally finding time for excursions to the beach and mountains, Baynham and I even pursed some outdoor adventures, namely rafting and camping trips.

With everything I had to keep myself busy, I fulfilled another dream of mine by enrolling in graduate school to earn a Masters in Business Administration. Since classes were held at the hospital late into evening after work, I frequently spent the night nearby at Carolyn's house. Over a two-year period, I made myself at home in Margaret's old bedroom, and my other social life took a backseat, by choice.

For different reasons, Dorothy's social life also lingered close to home. Her first marriage had ended in divorce, so as a single mother, she was trying to make it in this world and look after her child. During that same period, Carolyn was battling breast cancer, so surgery, dressing changes, chemotherapy, radiation, diagnostic tests, scans, blood work and doctors' appointments filled her days. Dorothy and I, therefore, took turns caring for her, while Carolyn was busy nurturing us in other ways.

"Sweetie, thank you so much for picking up dinner tonight," Carolyn said. Wheezing, she sank into her chair. "It was delicious," she added after taking another breath. I lifted her legs onto the ottoman.

"Absolutely," I said, noting that she was paler than usual and also seemed to tire more easily. "Not a problem and happy to do it." Thinking to myself how much Carolyn hated feeling bad, I observed as she lit up a post meal cigarette. Dorothy had told me that the doctors advised Carolyn to quit smoking, but she and I both knew it fell on deaf ears.

Instinctively, Carolyn read my mind and said, "Look sweetie, I'm going to die of something. I might as well die happy. And, by God, I plan on leaving the house feet first."

Busted by her invasion into my thoughts, I cracked up laughing. Even so, to comply with Dorothy's wishes, I refrained from smoking and partook in just two of the three vices usually shared with Carolyn. For the moment, however, I simply swirled my wine around and around in its glass while recalling a different time on the couch.

Quite a few years earlier, sitting in that same spot, I was heartsick and physically sick to my stomach. I was searching for answers: *How did I get so lost? Will I ever find true love? I have only forty dollars in my bank account and no longer a savings account. What am I going to do to make ends meet? How can I make more money? Who am I supposed to be? Where am I going?*

Now Carolyn was the one feeling nauseated, but from all of the drugs and chemo, and wondering if she could take one more day of the pain and discomfort. She had to be thinking, *Where am I going? What's going to happen to me? Who will look after my girls? Will they ever find true love?*

"I'm just so proud of you," Carolyn said, interrupting my thoughts, "of all my girls."

I smiled, knowing she was referring to the DGs. "How so?"

"You have such a remarkable friendship." Looking into my eyes, she said, "I know you have really been instrumental in keeping them all together." Her face was serious with all joking aside. "Promise me. Promise me that you will continue to look after each other, even after I am gone."

"I promise you that I will," I affirmed, making a pact that night before God and Carolyn.

"You have all been there for each other," she continued. "I've just loved watching you all grow up into beautiful women. And look at you now, accomplishing all that you set out to do in your professional careers. I'm just so proud. Please remember there is more to life than just your job. You need to find a balance between your work and a social life."

"Yeah, yeah, yeah," I injected. "I know. I know."

I knew. Carolyn was absolutely right. I was married to my career. I loved what I did. I was happy. I had found my calling, my joy and my passion caring for sick children; nevertheless, my job demanded the majority of my attention. I didn't have much time to focus on anything else. As a result, a gnawing void existed in my life that needed to be filled; a piece of my heart remained locked away. Still, I wasn't ready; I hadn't found the person who held the key.

Shifting the focus from me that night, I turned the tables and asked the questions. Carolyn reflected and pulled out all of her modeling photos and news clippings that I'd grown to know and love. She opened up, talking about her modeling work and family life, and shared that she was so glad she had a professional career before marrying Preston. She revealed that she was on the verge of being called an old maid but had chosen to ignore the social expectations of the times of marrying in one's early twenties and immediately starting a family. In her heart, she'd known she wasn't ready. She wanted to wait, experience life and settle down before having children of her own.

"Cheers!" Carolyn declared, leaning forward. "To living the dream! To following your dreams! To life!"

We toasted to life and took a sip of chardonnay. The ritual prompted me to recall an inspirational quote by Ghandi that I embraced: "Be the change you want to see in the world." I smiled knowing I was doing just that.

CHAPTER 9

Crossing Thresholds

A heavy cloak of humidity hung in the air on Monday afternoon, the day following Jennifer's graduation celebration. It mimicked my mood.

After taking the winding back roads to St. Joe's to visit Carolyn and then winding up and down the hospital's parking deck, I landed a spot. The day was scorching hot and I was tired of navigating, so I hopped onboard a golf cart for a complimentary ride rather than hiking in the heat to the front entrance. A perspiration glow had already emerged on my face, which was not uncommon. Quite honestly, being a woman on the downhill slide to approaching fifty, I would have appreciated the tiny breeze that the open cart ride provided almost any time of year. Grateful for the curb service, I profusely thanked my driver, an elderly gentleman wearing a vest that identified him as a hospital volunteer.

Extremely familiar with the layout of many hospitals in the area, I was particularly at home at St. Joe's. I had visited numerous times—for medical meetings, for Carolyn's and Preston's hospitalizations and surgeries, and even after the divorce, for Jeff's father's open heart surgery—so I easily found my way through the crowded lobby, past the coffee shop, to the main elevators, and up to the seventh floor.

Carolyn was in room 710. When the elevator doors parted, I stepped out and oriented myself to the unit. A beige directional sign on a sterile white wall indicated that I needed to turn left. Patient rooms were arranged in a semicircle around a nurses' station to provide the medical staff with a good line of sight and immediate access to anyone, and I went right to Carolyn's door. It was closed, so I peered through a rectangular window and waved to catch Dorothy's attention. She met me in the hallway, leaving two older men and a woman in the room to visit with her mother. Up close, I could see how swollen and bloodshot Dorothy's eyes had become in less than a day; she was physically, mentally and emotionally exhausted.

"Volunteers from Angel Flight just arrived," Dorothy commented.

Carolyn had served as a volunteer for the nonprofit organization, which provides free air transport for the medical needs of pediatric and adult patients, for over ten years. Every Wednesday she stuffed envelopes and answered phones. She loved the work and made many friends.

"She's hanging in there," Dorothy said. "She still can't eat or drink anything. She's receiving IV fluids for her dehydration and her belly is getting full of fluid again. I missed seeing the doctor this morning, but the nurse told me that we needed to start making hospice arrangements for Mom. I made an appointment with the hospice representative, and she's supposed to be here any time." Dorothy glanced at her watch.

Hospice. That meant that Carolyn's final days were quickly approaching. Her body was tired of fighting the cancer. Her organ systems were shutting down.

"Is there anything you need?" Uncontrollably, tears filled my eyes and streamed down my face.

Dorothy just shook her head in the negative. We were incapable of speaking at that point, so we cried and hugged each other. I rallied, however, to whisper in her ear. "You know how much I love you and Carolyn. I am here for you."

A doctor in a long white medical jacket approached and stood next to us, so Dorothy and I separated, regained our composure, and dried our eyes. In a manner that was routinely efficient, he retrieved the chart from a plastic holder affixed to the room next door, flipped through the pages and replaced it. With his mission established, he rapped his knuckles on the door and entered the patient's room.

"Since your Mom has guests, I don't want to interrupt them," I said, adding, "but please let her know I stopped by."

Dorothy gently grabbed the back of my arm. "Oh no, you don't! You're not getting off that easy. She'd be so *pissed* off if she knew you were here and didn't get the chance to see you. Go on into the room." Dorothy chuckled as she opened the door and pushed me across the threshold from behind.

I could feel her smile searing through the back of my blazer. Dorothy could tell that I was chickening out, afraid of the visit, scared to let her go, but knowing I'd regret it later if I left, she was not about to let me escape. She knew I'd brighten Carolyn's day and doing so would be a healing and beautiful gift to me.

CHAPTER 10
Couch Time with Carolyn Lesson #3:
Open Your Heart to Love

"Sweetie, show me. Show me," Carolyn repeated. "I can't wait to see it!" She positioned herself on her throne (the yellow couch, of course). A chilled glass of white wine sat within easy reach on the maple table, but the ceramic ashtray, lighter and smoky white haze that usually hung in the den were all absent. I couldn't believe that Carolyn had finally decided to stop smoking.

I placed the magazine's current issue, which sported a pink cover, on the ottoman in front of her, and she read aloud, "*Atlanta* magazine, February, 2004, 'Single in the City'."

Still inventorying our immediate surroundings, I also noticed the absence of the tobacco sticks. Carolyn, meanwhile, had taken her eyes off the magazine long enough to catch my observations. Before I could utter a word, she interjected, "Oh, don't congratulate me just yet. I still have them, hidden from plain view. I think it makes Dorothy happier for me to not be so open with my smoking." Lowering her wheezing voice to a whisper, as if Dorothy lurked in the shadows in the next room, she confided, "I still sneak a smoke every now and then."

"Of course you do!" I exclaimed. Laughingly, I shook my head, knowing that her vice was only out of view.

"Okay," she continued, indicating that the matter had been settled. "What page? What page?" Her hands flipped through the pages.

"Go to page eighty-seven," I said, watching for her reaction as she found the spot.

"Oh my goodness, sweetie! Carolyn, exclaimed, grabbing her readers from the basket. "There you are!" Holding the magazine close to her face, she hid all facial expressions from me. "Eight really cool unattached Atlantans." I could hear only her voice from behind the publication. "Oh, and there you are! Katie Hart, thirty-nine. Manager, Orthopedic Community Outreach, Children's Healthcare of Atlanta. A registered nurse and an aerobics instructor with an MBA, she co-founded a company called Smartmoovz that creates exercise videos for children. She once drove the Road Atlanta pace car in her first (and only) road rally. She snagged second place."

I found the whole thing absolutely surreal. It was weird to open a magazine and see my image staring back at me. Thirty-nine and still single, divorced for ten years, I was content with who I'd bloomed into being.

"I am just so proud of you," Carolyn proclaimed. "Oh … my … goodness!" At that point, she squealed. "Have your parents seen this yet?" she asked, placing the magazine in front of me on the coffee table.

"I mailed them a copy yesterday," I said. My parents still lived several states away, but they were closer since my dad, who was working for the same pharmaceutical company, had been relocated from California to New Hope, Pennsylvania.

"So how's dating life treating you?" Carolyn continued. "Tell me all of the details and don't skip a thing."

In my quasi-quest for Mr. Right, I continued to net Mr. Alright and Mr. Not Right. All the while, I valued Carolyn's wisdom about love, men and relationships, so I willingly shared my dating stories—the good, the bad, and the ugly ones. She, in turn, probed and reveled in the details, refusing to settle for simple *yes* or *no* questions.

"There are just so many fish in the sea," Carolyn said, somehow making a string of clichés sound wise and original. "Just take charge and cast your net. Listen to your heart. Your heart will tell you if he's a keeper or not," she continued, using both hands for emphasis while she talked around the lit cigarette in her mouth. (Carolyn had made me promise not to tell Dorothy where she kept them hidden.) She further insisted that I let go and have fun in life no matter where the journey led me.

As for the fun, recounting the details of my dating experiences provided plenty of entertainment for Carolyn. I'll never forget how she'd clap her hands and laugh in a manner that sounded like a hoarse, guttural howl. Her favorite blind date story of mine caused her to convulse into wheezing laughter, followed by a hacking coughing spell and tears streaming down her face.

In regard to that occasion, I had been set up by one of the DGs (who will remain nameless) with a guy a few years younger than I. The DG insisted he was nice and gainfully employed in a good job with a national broadcasting company based in downtown Atlanta. Since this DG was also single at the time, I asked why she had not dated him. When she said "no chemistry," I should have seen the red flag and translated what she was actually telling me: *you are doing me a favor.* Nevertheless, I agreed to talk with him. After screening him over the phone, I said I'd have dinner with him—despite the fact that his voice was three octaves higher than my own. Another red flag went ignored.

When we met up at a local Mexican restaurant, I gave him every benefit of the doubt. At five feet, eight inches tall, he had a stocky build that needed more height. His dark eyes and wavy black hair weren't bad, but his voice was so high-pitched that if I were to close my eyes, I'd swear I was talking to a young girl.

Although I tried everything to dismiss the way the guy sounded and get to know him instead, it couldn't be ignored. His voice—I just couldn't get over the stark contrast between its girlish quality and the man-child sitting next to me. Also, soon after the complimentary glasses of water, chips, and salsa arrived, our conversation stalled out and spiraled downward to a complete halt. With nothing to divert my attention, I couldn't ignore his table manners or demeanor, which were boyish, but not in a cute way. He was immature.

He was definitely not a match for me, and during the date, I'd catch myself looking for the emergency exits. The better part of me, however, recalled Carolyn telling me just to relax and have fun with dating experiences. Thanks to her, I didn't dart for the door.

Okay. Relax. Give him a chance.

Maya Angelou's quote ("The first time someone shows you who they are, believe them.") came to mind, and as a firm believer in giving people a chance so they can show you who they really are, their authentic selves, I did just that. And so he did—show me his authentic self. I endured the dinner date as he raked the burrito, enchilada, rice and beans combo platter into his mouth.

I didn't need any other red flags when the third and final one shot up the pole. (By that time, I was already kicking myself for not opting for an exit strategy at *hello.*) This warning, however, was apparent to anyone who might have glanced at our table. Another deafening lull had emerged in the conversation after dinner, so he began pulling out a myriad of magic tricks from various pants pockets. His idea of entertainment ranged from extracting a giant quarter from behind my ear to performing rope and knot tricks and something with rubber bands. When numerous rubber bands began flying about the table, I was not only mentally checked out, but also frantic for the waitress to bring the check. With the snap of a finger and a plume of white smoke, I really wanted to do a magic trick of my own: a vanishing act.

All in all, he had what I politely called *weirdness*. He was so weird that I thought for sure I was getting punked by the DGs. Meanwhile, I could hear Carolyn offering more advice, as if she were sitting beside me at the table, only this time she was saying, *He's definitely not a keeper! Throw him back!*

For more than a fleeting moment, I desperately wanted to throw something at my dear girlfriend who had set us up, but to this day, believe it or not, the DG who initiated such a memorable experience still swears that she had no idea that he was that strange. *Yeah, right!*

After my date with the weird man-boy magician, I wasn't too eager for another setup—at least not by a friend. Online dating, which had newly emerged on the scene, provided better filters. Even more promising was the fact that Susan had met her husband Kevin online, and they were happily married.

While I had fun with the challenge of explaining the new dating technology to Carolyn, the concept grew on me because I was so busy at the hospital; I didn't have time to immerse myself in the social scene. Thus, not long after that not-so-magical date, I opened an account with a well-known dating site; however, I was turned off by the schmooze, the one-liners, the misspelled words, and the descriptive sizes of cars, houses, bank accounts and man parts. Discouraged, I resolved that love was just not in the cards for me at that time. I was happy and secure with who I was as a person, and as I prayed each night, I took comfort in knowing that my life was in God's hands. He had the grand plan. I wasn't in control. So I let go to let Him show me the way.

Just as I decided I would close my online dating account, one guy caught my attention. He didn't schmooze, drop one-liners, misspell words or talk about his car, house, bank account or man parts. For those reasons, Jeff was the only guy I chose to correspond with online.

I learned that Jeff was recently divorced and in search of finding his true love. During email exchanges, he shared that his father's family, clan MacLeod, originated from Scotland. In turn, he asked where my family was from. I responded that Mom's side, the Isensees, were of German descent, while I thought the Hart family was originally from Whales. Expressing relief (jokingly) to find out that Dad's family was not from the humpback or sperm variety, Jeff revealed his sense of humor. We immediately progressed to phone conversations, and then decided to meet for a blind date at a local Thai restaurant that we both happened to love.

At six-feet, three-inches tall, Jeff could not be mistaken for a boy, and he had plenty more for me to appreciate. He looked causal yet masculine in his Georgia Bulldog shirt, black jeans, and black cowboy boots, and his light brown hair was cropped short in a style fitting for a police officer. Softening the ruggedness, a smile beamed from his face, and hazel-grey eyes sparked from behind his wire framed glasses. There was just something special about him—his voice, his boots, and his demeanor—signaling he was someone I wanted to get to know.

As we became acquainted, I realized he possessed the qualities on my non-negotiable list of date traits—my blueprint to determine if he was Mr. Right, Mr. Alright, or Mr. Not Right— which I had formulated and memorized years earlier:

Believed in God. *Check.*

Loved his parents and family. *Check.*

Authentic. *Check.*

Interesting. *Check.*

Respectful. *Check.*

Polite. *Check.*

Smart. *Check.*

Funny. *Check.*

Confident. *Check.*

Established in his career and loved what he did. *Check.*

And, newly added but nonetheless important, he didn't know any magic tricks. *Check.*

Extra credit points were given for the Georgia Bulldog shirt, black boots, and his Masonic ring. My father, uncles and grandfathers were all Masons. Also, like my grandfathers on Mom's side, Jeff belonged to the Scottish Rite and the order of the Knights Templar. Based on my assessment, he was a good man, a really good man.

During our discovery session, however, my guard did go up once, when Jeff asked, "How long have you been divorced?"

My defenses took over. Tapping into my inner smartass, I answered, "I've been divorced for over ten years." Jokingly, I added, "I can be divorced for ten more."

Without skipping a beat, he replied, "Well, that's just fine. I'm not taking any applications for the next Mrs. Smith."

From that moment on, we were inseparable. When we had to leave the Thai restaurant because it was closing, we headed to Starbucks around the corner and drank coffee until they closed their doors. We talked about our lives, professions and divorces, and laughed the night away.

As God would have it, Jeff held the key to unlock my heart. I opened my heart up to love—to give love, to receive love, to being in love, to finding my true love—and the gnawing void disappeared.

Carolyn met him and agreed. "He's definitely a keeper," she pronounced. Jeff was Carolyn- approved, and that was it.

We met in October, and Jeff went home with me at Christmas to meet my family. On a snowy afternoon in January, he held a small back box in his lap as he called my dad to ask for my hand in marriage. Jeff proposed to me that night in the Thai restaurant at the very table where we had our first date.

In August, just ten months after our first date, we had a traditional Scottish-themed wedding at the Lawrenceville First United Methodist Church, complete with Celtic harp, bagpipes, the Lawrenceville Police Department Honor Guard, and all of the MacLeod clan's plaid trimmings. The reception in the Fellowship Hall immediately followed the ceremony. There were no limos, Town Cars, tour busses, coat closets, ambulances, paramedics, brown paper bags, or announced or unannounced deaths or injuries in the immediate family.

At last, when Dad and I danced together to "Daddy's Little Girl," I felt so blessed and loved, as we were surrounded by family, friends, Carolyn and the DGs. Jeff and I brought out the best in each other, and I was proud and excited to walk by his side for the rest of our lives. God sent Jeff, answering our prayers in His grand plan for us.

In awe of His glory and grace, I thought of a verse from the Bible: "Strength and dignity are her clothing and she smiles at her future." Proverbs 31:25.

CHAPTER 11

Couch Time in the Hospital

Not allowing me to escape before having a meaningful visit with her mom and my other mom, Dorothy ushered me into Carolyn's hospital room. First taking time to exchange proper introductions and handshakes with the Angel Flight visitors, I stepped beside Carolyn's bed and took her hand in mine. The absence of her signature red fingernail polish first caught my attention. Her long beautiful arms were also discolored and covered with blue, green, and yellow bruises; the white sheets and pale blue hospital gown only enhanced her ghostly pallor. Clearly, her body was frail; she had lost considerably more weight since Susie and I had visited in the past month, which made it all the more obvious that her abdomen was distended under the bed covers. She'd suffered with emphysema from all the years of cigarette smoking, so to assist her breathing, her head was elevated and a nasal cannula was in place, providing her with oxygen. Plastic bracelets encircled her delicate wrists. One was her hospital identification band. The other was a red band with bold, black letters: DNR.

I silently translated in my head. *Do Not Resuscitate.*

Three little letters told the medical staff that in the event Carolyn's condition declined—if, for example, she stopped breathing or her heart stopped beating—she did not want any lifesaving heroics performed. No medications. No machines. She was taking control of her disease. She wanted to manage her final days on her terms.

As I held her hand in mine, I looked into her pretty hazel-blue eyes and told her how much I loved her.

"I'm so glad you're here, sweetie," she said, breathless. She repositioned the clear plastic prongs of the nasal cannula back into both nares, and I leaned over to adjust the tubing that wrapped around her ears. I brushed her white hair off of her forehead and listened as she told me about all of the procedures she endured since being admitted to the hospital. The doctors had poked and prodded her. She'd had enough and couldn't stand it any longer.

I looked intently into her eyes and again said, "I love you very much."

Carolyn looked at me and patted the back of my hand. "Well, isn't that what it's all about anyway?" A spark ignited in her eyes, and she winked and smiled.

Struggling with each breath, wise Carolyn had summarized the meaning and purpose of life in eight words, one sentence. Life was all about love. Her words instantly reminded me of the Bible verse I had memorized as a child from 1 Corinthians 13:13: "And now abides faith, hope, love, these three; but the greatest of these is love."

As if submerged by a powerful wave of anger, bargaining and depression, I couldn't breathe. I needed to breathe. *Take a deep breath*, I told myself. *Don't cry or lose it here in front of Carolyn, Dorothy, her visitors. Be strong. Keep it together. Pull ... it ... together.* I wanted to scream. I wanted to pick her up in my arms and hug her and say that this isn't fair. I wanted to say she wasn't alone. I wanted to burst into tears and sob.

Suppressing the rage welling up inside me, I calmly managed to say, "Yes, it is."

Suddenly, I was slapped with a reality. This was going to be the last and most important Couch Time with Carolyn lesson. Through all of the years we sat together, talking, commiserating and confiding in each other, she was quietly teaching and molding me to become the woman she knew God created me to be. She was my angel on earth. I had changed for knowing her, for loving her, for caring for her.

I was coming apart at the seams, but somehow kept my composure and my grief contained until it was time to say my goodbyes. After explaining that I needed to get back on the road, I bolted for the ladies' room down the hall, closed and locked the door, sat down on the toilet, buried my head in my hands and just bawled. When I regained my composure, I gathered my belongings and pulled a paper towel from the dispenser to dry my eyes. First checking my face in the mirror for makeup streaks and mascara blotches, I emerged from the bathroom and ran into Dorothy. She was on her way to meet a hospice representative to make the final arrangements to take Carolyn home to die—home, where Carolyn really wanted to be.

I made my way back down the elevator and out through the standing-room-only crowded lobby. Once outside, I consciously decided to take a slow walk through the oppressive heat and humidity back to the car. On the way, I remembered something Carolyn had told me during a Couch Time session a few years earlier. Her final wish was to leave home "feet first."

I smiled, knowing she was going home to do just that.

CHAPTER 12

Connecting the Dots

It was Wednesday morning, three days since I'd last seen Carolyn at St. Joe's. I grabbed my phone to call Dorothy and check in.

"Grand Central Station," The female voice sang out on the other end of the phone.

"What the heck is going on?" I inquired while sipping my first cup of coffee. Nothing made my morning beverage taste better than my favorite purple Gwinnett Diva coffee mug, a gift from attending the Gwinnett United Way Women's Fashion Show held at Stone Mountain Park's Evergreen Conference Center three years earlier.

"Well, Mom's home, and I'm looking after her," Dorothy informed in a tone that was suddenly more matter-of-fact.

"Where are you now?" I asked, taking another gulp of mocha hazelnut java.

"I'm home," she said.

"At your house in Dunwoody?" I asked, confused.

"Nope," Dorothy clarified, "Lilburn. When I met with the lady from hospice, she recommended that I bring Mom to our house in Lilburn. She said it would make it easier for me to care for her so that I wouldn't have to drive back and forth between Dunwoody and Lilburn. I talked with Robert and Jennifer about it. Hospice delivered a hospital bed, wheelchair, bedside commode and an oxygen machine to the house on Monday afternoon. An ambulance service transported her to the house later that day after your visit. And, would you know, in typical Carolyn fashion, Mom flirted with the uniformed paramedics during the entire ride. After, Mom asked them which one drove the vehicle. When one of the guys confessed he was the driver, she chided him and told him he must have hit every pothole between St. Joe's and the subdivision." Dorothy laughed. "I told the paramedic that Mom was notorious for being a bossy in the car. The fact that she was strapped to the stretcher and hooked up on oxygen in the back of the ambulance didn't matter a bit."

We both chuckled at the thought of Carolyn toying with the young drivers. I'm sure it made their day memorable.

"What can I do for you?" I asked, getting back the serious issue at hand. "How can I help you and Carolyn?"

"You know, your timing is perfect," Dorothy quickly answered. "Jennifer's graduation ceremony is scheduled for this Thursday evening. Would you come over and take care of Mom so I can be with Jennifer?"

"Sure," I said without hesitation. "Of course, I will. I'd be happy to and am honored that you asked."

Dorothy explained that the hospice nurse came over every morning to check in on Carolyn and gave her a bath every other day, but the past two days at home had been tough on the primary caregiver/daughter, as well as on Robert and Jennifer. Nighttime was the hardest. Dorothy had tried sleeping in her bed upstairs with a baby monitor to listen for her mom, who was in the guest bedroom downstairs. That didn't work because she was still up every two hours checking on Carolyn.

When Dorothy mentioned the guest bedroom, my mind wandered to another person we associated with the room, also a strong personality: Aunt Dot. As the sister of Dorothy's father, she was Dorothy's aunt and namesake, and Carolyn's sister-in-law. Everyone affectionately referred to the guest bedroom as Aunt Dot's room because that's where she stayed when she visited for the holidays. I was also reminded of the confidence and compassion Dorothy exhibited in handling the strong-willed lady under tricky circumstances.

Aunt Dot, who resided in Rome, Georgia, was a true vintage Southern belle; a classic—meaning the "Frankly, my dear, I don't give a damn" variety, not the delicate flower type. Just five feet - something inches tall, she made up in might what she lacked in stature. On top of being well-traveled, she was highly involved in the Floyd County community. In fact, she put her love of classical music to work playing the violin in the Rome orchestra.

·Like many talented people, Aunt Dot was also eccentric. We politely described her as a "collector." (Nowadays, her addiction is referred to as hoarding.) She saved *everything*, and I mean every little thing, from tiny pieces of paper, bills, and newspapers to rubber bands and expired foods. She despised seeing anything go to waste, hated throwing anything into the trash. It was common knowledge not to eat anything from her refrigerator without checking the expiration dates if rank odors from strange bacterial growth didn't stop you.

After Aunt Dot's mother passed away, her mother's home, which had been vacant for months, needed cleaning before being put on the market to sell. Dorothy had the fun task of convincing Aunt Dot that the contents of the house needed to be cleared out. When Aunt Dot finally granted Dorothy approval to enter the place, the DGs were summoned to help Dorothy and Margaret.

A caravan of two cars carried Dorothy, Margaret, Susie, Carole, Robert and me up I-75 North to Rome. Susan, a.k.a. Baynham, was the only DG who couldn't join us on this exploit; she was too busy with her young girls, Katie and Rebecca. Incidentally, Carole and her husband Kurt were the proud parents of Sarah and Adam. Susie, consumed by kindergartners and exhaustion, was contemplating if she had the energy to find the man of her dreams at that point in her life. I was continuing my quest to find true love, although usually joking that my knight in shining armor had fallen off his horse, bent the hinges in his knee guards and was having difficulty walking in his attempts to find me. The quest for love slowed. God was teaching me a lesson in patience.

The moment we unloaded the cars and barged in with our cleaning supplies, brooms, mops, rubber gloves and trash bags, I noticed a large steel dumpster at the end of the driveway by the garage. This was what my now and forever husband would call a *clue*. I next looked at the twenty-five count box of trash bags in my hands and shook my head.

This was going to be a long day.

My assumptions were correct. The tiny white house located in a charming, established neighborhood was, in reality, a museum for lost and hidden treasures. Under normal circumstances, a crew would have requested days or weeks to excavate each relic and disinfect every surface, but Dorothy said our job was to work quickly. Aunt Dot, well into her nineties, loathed the thought of having all of us in her mother's house because we might throw away something of value. Still driving and proving to be someone no one wanted to cross, she was going to swing by to check in on us at some point during the day. We had no idea what Aunt Dot might do when she caught us in the act, but we obediently put our lives on the line and followed Dorothy's orders. As soon as she assigned us our respective rooms, we split up and began the cleaning process.

Margaret and I were sent to battle the kitchen. Prepared for combat, we donned our rubber gloves and had face masks ready to wear in case we ran across a despicably smelly item. A three-hundred-sixty-degree reconnaissance of the territory helped us grasp the scope of our mission, and we agreed to break down the project into three phases. Phase one began with the refrigerator. We swore with a pinky promise not open any containers that would require notification to the Centers for Disease Control that we'd unleashed a new biochemical hazard into the world.

Starting out, Margaret held the black plastic trash bag while I removed all of the food crammed on the top shelf. I moved down, repeating the extraction process, until all shelves and compartments were eradicated of any evidence of food, living or expired. The wire shelves were removed and cleaned, and I wiped down the walls with a water and bleach mixture, but we sadly concluded that no amount of bleach could restore the avocado green unit, circa 1960, to anything close to attractive.

Calling a truce with the refrigerator, we moved onto phase two: the kitchen cabinets.

While Margaret launched an attack on the far right cabinets, I tackled the ones on the far left. Our plan was to meet in the middle over the sink. Following clear directives from Dorothy, we saved all items in good working condition and tossed everything else. In the meantime, Robert, serving as our trash man, remained on constant patrol. Going room to room, he removed all full trash bags, heaving them one by one into the giant steel dumpster outside. Needless to say, as the day progressed and the dumpster filled with black plastic bags, we grew more anxiously alert for the arrival of Aunt Dot.

Margaret and I pressed on, but we were not prepared for how daunting it would be to clean out those cabinets. Her findings of glassware, plates, pots and pans, however, could not have been as overwhelming as the canned and dry goods I uncovered. With each squeaky metal door I flung open, I found stacks and stacks and stacks of canned soups, fruits and vegetables, complete with various assortments of dried beans, pasta and boxes of gelatin. Some of the containers had logos and brands that I hadn't seen for years, and their expiration dates proved such items were never intended to exist beyond 1985, 1998, 19 ... (smudged).

When I finally got my plastic gloved hands around the last can of peaches, it wouldn't budge. I attempted to shake it loose with one hand, then both hands. It still wouldn't move. The can of peaches had somehow fused itself to the shelf, refusing to be dislodged and thrown into the giant collection container in the driveway. I had met my match in the *mother* of all steel cans. With no other choice, I laughed as I climbed up on the counter to get more leverage, and that's when Margaret came over to help.

The two of us, wrestling with that one last can, were bound and determined to win the battle. Our ridiculous effort had us laughing so hard that Robert came over to see what all of the fuss was about. At that point, we stepped away.

One Can of Peaches – 1 versus Two Girls – 0

Conceding for the moment, we decided to let the man prove that he could succeed. Robert, struggling to set the can free, was soon muttering inaudible words of encouragement (or something like that) to himself. He, too, proved to be unsuccessful and struck out.

One Can of Peaches – 2 versus Two Girls and a Guy – 0

By now, the entire crew had amassed in the kitchen to cheer on the peach extraction project. During its years of clinging to some kind of existence beyond its intended shelf life, that can of peaches decided to fuse itself to the metal. Mimicking Aunt Dot, it refused to let go.

I rummaged through the remaining kitchen drawers to find a hammer, a screwdriver, or any kind of implement that could be used as leverage to pry the last remaining relic from the kitchen. I located a flat head screwdriver—*perfect!*—and proceeded to surgically remove the base of the can from the shelf. Finally, the can began to pry lose, pulling all the paint off the shelf that surrounded it. With a giggle, a wiggle and a tug, the can was freed.

Now, at that point, I became even more perplexed. Comparing the weight of the peaches in my left hand with the screwdriver in my right, I realized the screwdriver was heavier. I shook the can and nothing. No sound of any liquid substance inside. Inspecting the top and the bottom, I knew that can had never been opened. It didn't have a pull top, so I used an electric can opener to unlock the mystery. Unbelievably, the little sucker was completely empty. It had lived on the kitchen shelf for so long that the expired contents had decomposed and evaporated.

What a stubborn empty can of peaches! I thought, as I hurled its remainders into a plastic trash bag. *Two points.* Just as I was dancing in celebration of my winning two-pointer shot, my cheering section and I observed a silver car coming up the driveway. The music in my head screeched to a stop and I froze, along with everyone else.

Someone shouted out, "Oh, shit! Aunt Dot's here!"

For a few nanoseconds, sheer pandemonium erupted. We scattered like leaves to the wind, and in a mad scramble, trash bags were hurled out the door, kicked under beds and shoved into closets. Open cabinet doors and drawers were rapidly closed, concealing all evidence of the monumental cleaning project underway.

The sound of the car door slamming shut made us turn into little soldiers. Lining up in the living room, we snapped to attention and stood in silence as we observed the painstakingly slow yet imminent opening of a white lacy parasol. Aunt Dot, who detested the sun, made sure a ray never kissed her face. Thus, she was completely covered by the parasol. We couldn't see her, so we watched it bob up and down as Aunt Dot proceeded up the driveway, coming closer and closer as she made her way past the long living room window to the kitchen.

When our general landed on the back porch steps, she closed her sun protector, also a handy weapon, and raised her nose in the air as if to inspect the cleanliness level of the job we were doing. I can only assume that the percentage of bleach to window cleaner and all-purpose surface cleaner to oxygen levels met with her exacting standards because Aunt Dot did not raise her weapon. Instead, she carefully entered the kitchen and cautiously looked around.

To expedite the inspection of our work and, in effect, minimize her comprehension of our impact on the battleground, Dorothy burst forth from the lineup and ushered Aunt Dot quickly around the house. All along, we never broke rank. We remained silently in the line we'd formed in the living room with our rubber gloved hands behind our backs. Like any attentive soldier, however, I listened for signs of hostility from the other side and overheard Aunt Dot saying how she hated to see anything discarded and thrown away. Remarkably, Dorothy, in her angelic voice, assured her aunt that all items were individually inspected by her certified team of house cleaners. She further reiterated that she was supervising the entire cleanup project, everything was going very well, and nothing of value was being tossed carelessly into that horrible dumpster. A flip of her hand towards the canister in the driveway emphasized her point, as if the beastly object had been tamed and would do no harm.

Satisfied with what she saw, heard, and smelled, Aunt Dot raised her closed parasol into the air like a baton with her right hand and exited the premises with orders for us to "carry on." Like a housekeeper's drill team, we raised our yellow plastic-gloved hands and waved good-bye to her in unison. Aunt Dot popped open the parasol that caused her to disappear from view, and bobbed back down the driveway to her car.

As I watched, I couldn't help myself from wondering, *Who still makes parasols like that anymore? Could Mary Poppins be missing hers?*

Dorothy was impressive in that situation. She remained calm and composed as she lovingly took care of her Aunt Dot. Unbeknownst to us, the mission was preparing Dorothy and the DGs for a more important battle: Carolyn's final fight with cancer.

CHAPTER 13

My Last Couch Time with Carolyn

Carolyn spent the day of Jennifer's high school graduation in Aunt Dot's room, where she slept in a hospital bed that was positioned parallel to a window. Warm summer breezes blew outside, causing the branches of a tree to brush lazily against the panes. The abrupt arrival of summer, Jennifer's milestone, and Carolyn's presence in Aunt Dot's room had me wishing life would slow down. Every change seemed to convey a loss, so I concentrated on what was permanent.

Aunt Dot had recently passed. The memories and stories of her, however, along with some of her treasured belongings, were kept and cherished. Carolyn would be next. Looking almost the same as when I had last visited her on Monday, she appeared to be sitting upright in the bed. Dressed in another light blue hospital gown, she was still wearing her wedding rings on her clinched fingers and her watch adorned her left wrist, but the DNR bracelet remained in place, too. And she wasn't sitting; the bed was elevated.

Carolyn's gown was unfastened in the back, and it draped over her tiny withered shoulders. A closer look revealed hands that were swollen and bruised, and when Dorothy pulled back Carolyn's blanket and sheet to expose her legs, ankles and feet, I could see they were discolored and swollen as well. Her toes were painted her favorite red, but the polish was chipping off. Caring for Carolyn had been reduced to keeping her comfortable. From the swelling and the scant amounts of dark, amber-colored urine in the collection bag beside her bed, I knew her kidneys and liver had failed; the fluid in her abdomen had moved into her extremities.

Gurgling water accompanied a *shish-too* sound as the machine behind her bed delivered humidified oxygen into Carolyn's nose through the nasal cannula. "Yesterday the oxygen tube disconnected itself from the machine," Dorothy revealed. "I was grateful that the hospice nurse was here to help reconnect the tubing. I wouldn't have known what to do." When the nasal cannula slipped from her mother's nose the first time, the lack of oxygen to her body caused the tips of her fingers and toes to turn blue and black. That, too, had been a frightening experience for Dorothy.

Both mother and daughter had surrendered to reality; appearances no longer mattered. Numerous supplies—a roll of paper towels, a box of tissues, a blanket, hospice brochures and folders, and a tray of new urinary catheters—were displayed across the guest bed. An emesis basin and a large serving tray full of prescription medications and ointments waited at the foot of the bed. A bedside commode took up space nearby.

"Mom insisted on using the bathroom on the first night," Dorothy recounted. "It was such a struggle lifting her and helping her to the toilet. Mom said she felt an urge to urinate, but I kept telling her that she had the catheter in place and she didn't need to get out of bed. She wanted to try anyway."

"Did the doctors prescribe any medicine for the bladder spasms?" I asked. As a nurse, I knew that the urinary catheter combined with the fluid in Carolyn's abdomen was creating the sensation that she had a full bladder.

"Yes, they did," Dorothy said, picking up one of the golden-colored prescription bottles "It's this one."

I recognized the name brand Ditropan. The prescription medication that eased bladder spasms had been a tremendous relief to some of my pediatric patients, such as those with spina bifida.

"Mom hasn't wanted to use the bathroom anymore since Monday night," Dorothy added, conveying another layer of bad news.

Three days, I counted to myself.

"I also noticed today that she has lost her swallowing reflexes," my friend continued. "She isn't able to chew and can only sip small—I mean *tiny*—amounts of Ensure-coated ice chips. I offer them to her when she wakes from a nap, and she holds her hand up when she has had enough."

I nodded, showing I understood to give Carolyn only the scant amount of fluid that she could sip.

Having reviewed Carolyn's condition, we left her alone to rest and headed to the kitchen. Since Aunt Dot had no children of her own, her estate had passed to her nieces, Dorothy and Margaret, when she died. Dorothy used some of her inheritance to renovate the kitchen with tiled flooring, granite countertops, updated cabinets and new ovens. Another portion of the money sent Jennifer on a high school trip to Switzerland and Italy.

Dorothy pointed out a legal pad and a spiral bound notebook like the ones we used in school. Handwritten schedules, medication doses, and "last administered" dates and times next to each medicine filled the pages. Phone numbers to hospice's on-call service appeared prominently on the top sheet.

"Her next doses of Dilaudid and Ativan are in an hour," Dorothy said. The Dilaudid, a narcotic, would manage Carolyn's pain. Although Ativan was a common anti-anxiety drug, it was prescribed for Carolyn and other cancer patients to ease nausea and vomiting. "Since she can't swallow the pills, I have been crushing them between two spoons and gently sprinkling the powder onto the inside lining of her lower lip. The hospice nurse told me the meds will be absorbed quickly that way and that I could offer to follow the meds with sips—I mean *minuscule* sips—of water, ice or Ensure. If some of the liquids dribble out of her mouth, I have a washcloth at the end of the bed to wipe her face."

Lingering decorations from the graduation party, held just four days earlier, seemed frozen in time, as if from another era. Confetti clung to the kitchen tablecloth alongside hospice folders and brochures. The flower bouquet that had looked so vibrant in its crystal vase had wilted, scattering petals on the counter. From the kitchen I could see that the red tablecloth still adorned the dining room table, and the designated drink station, complete with plastic cups and soda bottles, remained intact on the screened porch.

Oblivious to my visual inspection of the premises, Dorothy pulled a white cardboard box wrapped in red tape from the top shelf of the refrigerator. I counted at least ten medication stickers on the lid; accordingly, the box held an impressive array of pills, liquids and suppositories.

"This is the emergency medication kit," Dorothy announced. Her tone was somber. "It contains liquid Morphine for Mom's breakthrough pain. Normally, they said, this medicine is clear. However, the pharmacy dyed the liquid light blue so it wouldn't be confused with any other clear fluid, like water. Atropine is to be given when the oral secretions get to be too much. Phenergan is for any nausea and vomiting. I also have these medications in suppository form in case she can no longer take them orally."

Dear God, I don't want to have to use the emergency medicine kit during Dorothy's absence. Amen.

She placed all of the medications back into the box and returned the kit to the top shelf of the refrigerator. We reviewed last-minute checklists, making sure Dorothy showed me where she kept the front door key and that I had her cell phone number in my phone. Check, check and double check.

"Please don't answer the phone," Dorothy said, tossing out a few more instructions as they came to mind. "Just let it go to voicemail. Robert will come straight home from work. He'll go in and speak to Mom, but that is all he can manage to do at this time."

After confirming directions to the World Congress Center, where Jennifer's graduation ceremony was taking place, we went through a final checklist together.

"Car keys?" I asked.

"Check," she responded.

We continued our Qs and As, confirming that Dorothy had her cell phone, graduation ticket and camera, but when I asked about parking money, she didn't say *check*.

"Oh, crap!" Dorothy cringed with clenched fists. "I don't have any cash. I need to run by the ATM."

"No need," I interjected, opening my turquoise wallet and handing her cash for the road. I jokingly said, as all parents tell their children, "Now, don't spend it all in one place."

At last, I said something to make Dorothy laugh! Feeling a bit more like herself, she also remembered to shed her Crocs and step into her slingback black pumps before saying goodbye. Listening to the garage door open and close, I found myself alone with Carolyn and the machine that kept her alive with a constant gurgle and *shish-too*.

I returned to Aunt Dot's room and stood beside Carolyn. She weakly picked up her head, so I leaned over the bed and explained that I would be staying with her that afternoon. Her lids were heavy, but she opened her eyes. Accustomed to her beautiful, hazel blues, I saw glazed, milky white orbs instead. They were mirrors, revealing just a shadow of the wisecracking woman that use to laugh and carry on with me. The oxygen tickled her nose, so she reflexively lifted her right hand in an attempt to scratch it. Dorothy had told me she would do that. I waited expectantly, but Carolyn only muttered incoherently. Her head then dropped and her heavy eyelids closed once again. While I had cared for many critically ill children over the course of my clinical nursing career, Carolyn was not only my first adult patient, but she was also someone I knew like my own mother. And she was dying before my eyes. There was nothing more to be done for her but simply make her comfortable. There were no more miracles of modern medicine to help her.

To cope with the prognosis, I automatically went into nurse mode. I checked the electrical equipment and the oxygen tank to be sure they were plugged into the wall and the tubes correctly connected. I lifted the sheets to make sure nothing was binding her arms or legs. I made sure the urinary catheter tubing wasn't kinked or pinched off by the hospital bed rails, inhibiting the flow of urine into the collection bag. Everything was in good working order to keep Carolyn comfortable.

I pulled up a chair and sat beside her. Holding her hand in mine, I said a prayer. *God is surely in this place*, I thought. I was a changed woman for knowing her, and in that very moment, praying beside Carolyn, I felt our Couch Time sessions coming to a crescendo.

Carolyn's life was coming to a close, but Jennifer's graduation ceremony symbolized the start of a new chapter. Two worlds— one ending and one beginning—were colliding. The relationships Carolyn shared with us were also reversed. For years, she had been the one to look after her family, her daughters and me, making us feel special and loved. It was now Carolyn's time to be cared for in a house filled with family and love, in room filled with family photographs and fond memories.

Carolyn, Dorothy and Margaret were surrounded by love. They had one another and the DGs. And we were there for one another. Always had been, always would be. Our love for each other sustained us. Carolyn knew how much I loved her, and I knew that her love had prepared me for that evening. It would be my last Couch Time with Carolyn session and the pinnacle of all of her life lessons. Thinking back to the hospital visit just four days earlier, I felt blessed to have told Carolyn how much I loved her. In turn, her departing words would resonate with me forever. *We'll isn't that what it's all about, anyway? Love.* I would always be in awe of her infinite wisdom and grace.

An hour later, I made sure she received her medications. Another hour passed and Carolyn came out of her slumber. I leaned over and softly said, "Carolyn, it's Katie. I'm staying with you this evening."

Carolyn looked up, and the milky white haze in her eyes cleared. "I know," she responded before closing eyes and drifting back to sleep.

I continued to sit beside Carolyn, but I eventually had to look away from the bruised, bluish hand I held. Gazing around the room, I noticed a picture of her husband Preston on the mahogany dresser behind her bed. The handsome man with perfect white teeth and crystal blue eyes had been photographed in a sailor's hat and shirt for his military headshot. He was wearing glasses, but the frames only enhanced his features.

The sound of the automatic garage door opening, followed by heavy footsteps climbing the basement stairs, broke my trance. When Robert appeared, I stood to give him a hug, debriefing him on Carolyn's status.

He picked up her hand, placing it in his, and said, "Carolyn, I'm home." Pausing only for a moment, he gently let go and turned away. We left the bedroom and went to the kitchen.

"I am so happy you are here to help Dorothy and me out today," Robert said. He audibly sighed with relief as he retrieved a bottle of Scotch from the liquor cabinet.

Father's helper, I thought to myself.

"You want one, too?" Robert asked, reaching for a glass.

"No, thanks, I'm on duty," I said, using air quotes for *on duty*.

I sat on the barstool listening to Robert explain how rough the recent change of events had been on Dorothy, Jennifer and him. I continued listening as he talked about Carolyn, his mom battling dementia, his work, and his activities at church. He was such a good husband to Dorothy. The two had met each other on a blind date, set up by a mutual friend from their Methodist church a few years earlier. Dorothy had found her true love. I knew she felt happy and secure over her new future with Robert.

When a look of exhaustion cascaded across his face, Robert decided to get comfortable and unwind from work by watching television in the den. I excused myself and let him know I'd be sitting in Aunt Dot's room with Carolyn if he needed anything.

While I'd brought a book to read, I found myself unable to concentrate on the words. Instead, I monitored the oxygen machine. Watching Carolyn's chest slowly rise and fall with every labored breath going into and out of her body, I caught myself breathing to the rhythm of the machine. In addition to our breathing, all of the minor details of our surroundings became magnified. I noticed, for instance, that with the darkening sky, the leafy branches that pressed against the window now appeared in hues of gray and black. Evening had settled in.

Once again, the automated garage door opened and closed, interrupting my meditative state. The clipping sound of high heels coming up the basement steps confirmed that Dorothy was home.

She looked in and saw that her mom was still asleep, so Dorothy and I joined Robert in the den. I had hoped that the graduation would be a joyful experience for her, but Dorothy came home frustrated over the disruptive behavior of family members and friends as graduates were announced. "They would stand, cheer, hoot and holler, despite the stern warning they all received from the principal, who asked them before the commencement ceremony began to hold their applause until all of the students' names had been called," Dorothy scoffed. "The parents and other relatives who sat around me were even talking on their cell phones during the students' speeches. It was so inconsiderate and rude! People weren't being respectful of each other."

I didn't blame her one bit. It was amazing how cell phones had changed people's etiquette and social behavior, even during sacred milestones, like weddings, funerals and graduation ceremonies. We both concurred that if these events were witnessed by Emily Post, she'd have a complete stroke.

We were, however, happy about one handy technology. Dorothy had taken excellent photos of Jennifer walking across the graduation stage in her cap and gown. Someone also captured a picture of the mom and daughter together before the graduate removed her ceremonial attire and left for a celebratory dinner with her dad. The photo of Dorothy beside Jennifer in her red and yellow school colors, which were similar to the crimson and gold we had worn thirty years ago at Dunwoody High School, gave me a flashback to that time. Only the faces and hairstyles had changed. In that moment, I glimpsed the evolution of a generation.

The circle of life continues, I thought.

Jennifer's graduation year also serendipitously coincided with our thirtieth DHS class reunion. As it turned out, Susie and I were in the midst of planning the party, slated for the coming month at the Dunwoody Marriott. Susie was on the steering committee and I opted to help out with decorations, and all of the DGs had been planning for months to attend in full force. We even decided to have a girls' getaway, leaving the husbands at home and spending the weekend at the hotel. Our hotel rooms were reserved and our tickets were purchased for the Friday and Saturday night events. We couldn't wait to reconnect with former classmates and spend the weekend together like we did in our younger and single days.

Thirty years of life experiences, though, had allowed our DG relationships to go much deeper. We were changed from the experiences we have shared together, which also prepared and brought us to a new level of maturity and understanding about what was really important in this lifetime. Life is about the simple things—creating memories, experiences, faith, family and friends. A rich collection of the simple things supported and sustained us, enabling us to endure the tough times, even facing the immediate reality of losing Carolyn.

Before I left that evening, Dorothy accompanied me to Aunt Dot's room, where I would see Carolyn for the last time as an angel on earth. Her breathing had become more labored than when we had last looked in on her. God would soon take her as his angel in heaven. She was still sleeping, but I gently placed her hand in mine, kissed her on the forehead and said, "I love you, Carolyn."

CHAPTER 14
The Call

The Memorial Day weekend was upon us, and Jeff and I awoke to a sunny, humid Saturday morning. I looked at myself in the bathroom mirror and washed my face with a cold washcloth. My eyes were red and swollen from crying through *War Horse*, the movie we had watched the night before about a beloved battlefield horse during World War I. I was a total blubbering basket case through the entire film. If I had known the storyline before going in, I would have chosen a comedy or something a bit more lighthearted to unwind to after a difficult week. As I brushed my teeth, I overheard the weather forecaster on FOX 5 predicting temperatures in the mid-90s all weekend long. The last week of May was going to be a scorcher.

The sweet aroma of bacon—*yum!*—greeted me on my way downstairs. Jeff was frying up some thick slices in my Grandma Gigi's cast iron skillet, our prized possession. Strips of bacon sizzled, popped and crackled in the pan. The skillet contained at least ninety years of seasonings, so we followed the cardinal rule of cleaning it only with scalding hot water, and after, thoroughly drying and resealing the surface with oil and locking in all of the flavorful goodness on a heated stove top or in the hot oven. We never exposed the skillet to the tiniest drop of soap.

I assisted by scrambling up cheese eggs to accompany the bacon. While using the whisk, I chuckled at the memory of a story Jeff's brother told about a classroom experience he had while attending the Le Cordon Bleu culinary college in Atlanta. An instructor had asked the students, "Where did bacon come from?" He expected someone to give the correct anatomical location on the pig. Nevertheless, one student shouted out, "Heaven!" Smelling the undeniable aroma of bacon, I had to agree with him one-hundred percent.

Jeff and I sat down, said the blessing and ate breakfast. Before washing up the dishes, we collectively developed our weekly grocery list. Jeff loved doing the grocery shopping and I, well, let's just say, not so much. I preferred to shop with a directive and a purpose. It was a task to be fulfilled and crossed off my to-do list. Jeff, on the other hand, shopped aisle by aisle, making sure he conducted price comparisons while gathering every item on the list. He also loved to look for new food items on the shelves and found the whole experience totally relaxing and enjoyable. I didn't. My mission was to get in and get out of the grocery store.

Check. Done. Move on.

I then headed downstairs to the basement office. The Dunwoody High reunion was exactly four weeks away, and I needed to scan graduation photos from the DHS yearbook to a computer file I was creating for reunion name badges. After, I compared the nineteen photos in my file to the nineteen names on the RSVP list I had to date. Yup, the names and numbers matched. With that accomplished, I picked up my phone to call Dorothy at the same moment it vibrated in my hand and lit up with Dorothy's name on the screen. Sensing she had news, I glanced at the clock on the wall: 10:15 A.M.

"Oh, God!" I muttered to myself and answered.

"Well," she began, but then came a pregnant pause, followed by silence and a deep breath.

Brace yourself, I thought, *here it comes.*

"Mom passed away last night," Dorothy somberly continued. "She went peacefully. I was at her side and then walked into the kitchen to get some more pain medication. When I came back, I noticed she had stopped breathing. It was very peaceful," she reiterated.

I couldn't stop the flow of tears that welled up in my already puffy eyes and overflowed down my cheeks. I tried wiping them away in a futile attempt.

"I'm so sorry, Dorothy," I managed to say. "She was so fortunate to have you by her side. You were a loving and caring daughter. You have taken such great care of her. You were there for her until the end."

As soon as my words stopped, it began. The ugly cry—the one where you can't see and can't breathe; your nose runs; the nasal cavities and sinuses swell and slam shut. You can only mouth breathe to prevent yourself from passing out. I'm crying and I hear Dorothy crying. A few minutes pass before we regain our composure.

Dorothy is the one to continue the conversation. "Margaret is driving in from Texas and bringing the kids. She'll stay at Mom's house. The funeral will be at Patterson's by Oglethorpe University, where we had Dad's service. We can't have Mom's ceremony until mid-week," Dorothy added. "Evidently, there is a backlog of services with the Memorial Day weekend and we have to wait until Wednesday."

I was perplexed. It was Saturday and Carolyn had to wait until Wednesday for her funeral service.

"What?" I asked. "Who knew funeral homes had a holding pattern like planes flying into Hartsfield-Jackson International Airport on a busy day!"

Dorothy laughed heartily at my comment and said, "I know! Really?" We were both envisioning a line of caskets wrapped around the building, waiting to get into Patterson's. We came to the same conclusion: *It is what it is.*

"Mom wanted to be cremated," she continued. "I'm not sure about having a viewing. I just don't know. I'll think about that later. At least I have the funeral scheduled for Wednesday afternoon at 2:00 P.M."

I asked Dorothy what she needed help with on that day and in the days that followed.

"Just activate the DG phone tree and let everyone know of Mom's passing and about the funeral arrangements," she said.

"Got it," I replied. "Anything else?"

"No, not right now," she said. "Jennifer is pretty upset. She was out with her friends last night and felt bad that she wasn't there when her grandma passed away."

"Well, the memories of the times she had with her grandma will always be with her," I offered and Dorothy agreed.

"Jennifer and I are driving to Mom's house later today to pick out her outfit; the one she'll be cremated in." Dorothy then laughed as she said, "When I spoke with Margaret, she wanted me to make sure that I had Mom properly clothed because, Lord knows, Mom didn't want to meet Jesus buck naked!"

The thought of Carolyn meeting Jesus and St. Peter at the Pearly Gates with just a big ol' smile made me laugh out loud right along with her.

"And," Dorothy continued, "she hated panty hose. So, if I put her in panty hose, she'll come back to haunt me."

"Yes, yes, she would!" I cracked up knowing how much Carolyn and the rest of us hated wearing panty hose, especially on hot and humid days in Atlanta, or on any day for that matter.

"I … I can't thank you enough for looking after Mom on Thursday night," Dorothy said, her tone serious again. I also heard trembling in her voice when she added, "I was trying to figure out how to get to Jennifer's graduation ceremony and look after Mom."

"Dorothy, you were trying to balance two things: one, being Jennifer's mother, and two, being Carolyn's daughter. On Thursday, you needed to be Jennifer's mom, to be there for Jennifer on her important day. I'm so glad I could be there to help you."

By that time, we were both sobbing and on the verge of releasing the ugly cry again. I dug deep and managed to tell her how much I loved her and that I would do anything for her. I thanked her for letting me care for her mom. We were all there for Carolyn in her final days. She was never alone; she was always surrounded by her loved ones. She also departed this world on her terms: She left home "feet first" just like she always wanted.

As soon as we collected ourselves once more and said our good-byes, I activated the DG phone tree. Susie's name popped up first, but I should have called her last because she answered sleepily. The kindergarten teacher cherished the weekend mornings that she could sleep in past 6:00 A.M.

My next call went to Carole. Her husband Kurt answered and informed me that Carole was out running errands, but he expected her home any time. I went ahead and gave him the news and asked that he have her call me when she returned.

Next on the list was Susan, a.k.a. Baynham. When she answered, I could tell she was in the middle of doing something important, so I kept it short, sweet and businesslike. "Dorothy's mom passed away last night," I blurted out.

"Okay," Baynham said, confirming receipt of the message.

"The funeral will be held at Patterson's Funeral Home by Oglethorpe University on Wednesday at 2:00 P.M. Not sure about a viewing," I added. "I will keep you posted if that changes."

"Okay," she replied again.

"Please let your mother know," I urged. Dorothy and Susan had grown up in the same neighborhood; their houses were right around the corner from each other. They had been friends since kindergarten. Mrs. Baynham and Carolyn were friends, too.

"Mom will be back by then," Baynham pointed out. That was her way of indicating to me that her mom was not at her home in Dunwoody, and wherever else she was in the world at that moment, she would be back in time to attend the funeral. To anyone else listening to our phone exchange, Baynham's response would come across as a little cold, but knowing her like I do, she was a private woman of few words who didn't care much for phone chatter.

"Okay, great," I concluded. "Thanks."

"Anything else?" Baynham was winding down the conversation.

"Uh, no," I responded.

We said our good-byes and that was that. Short, sweet and to the point—that was Baynham.

I gathered my thoughts. Whom to call next? My parents, Jeff's parents and my sister Julie. I accounted for the checklist of people I had to contact that morning and gave Jeff the task of calling his parents, who lived just fifteen minutes from our home. I knew his mom would cry when he told her the news and she did. She loved Dorothy. Dorothy's genuinely heartfelt, empathetic nature became evident to her a few years earlier when my dear friend sat with us in the waiting room while Jeff's dad underwent open heart surgery at St. Joe's. Of course, Jeff's parents said they would attend the funeral, and his mother also insisted on making some kind of casserole for the family. Then she deliberated about of what kind of casserole to make. Jeff reassured his mother that whatever she decided would be just fine as long as it could be frozen. Both agreed that the "freezability" quotient of the dish was of key importance and the means by which to rank the quality of any funeral food.

While they deliberated casseroles, I tried calling my parents, followed by my sister Julie. Julie and Dorothy's sister Margaret were the same age and in the same grade at Dunwoody High School. My parents weren't home and neither was my sister, so I left messages that relayed the news about Carolyn's passing and her funeral arrangements.

My Mom was the first to call back. I knew that I'd begin crying as soon as I opened my mouth and that I would take her down with me and she'd be crying, too. I did. She did. We did. I told her the stories of the previous days and the events that transpired. We talked about sending flowers on behalf of the family and agreed that Jeff and I would handle those details with Huff's Flowers, our local florist.

My sweet husband took on the duty of ordering the flowers as his Tuesday to-do task. He even sent himself a reminder email since the florist was closed for the holiday weekend. I asked Jeff to divide the order into two potted flower gardens, one from the Smiths squared (as in two families) and the other from my parents and my sister's family. That way, Dorothy and Margaret would each have a planted garden to take home with them after the funeral. I personally thought that long lasting planted arrangements versus fresh cut flowers provided a sweeter reminder of departed loved ones. I loved sustainability, even in funeral arrangements.

Jeff departed for the grocery store and I started on my domestic goddess chores. When he returned, I went to the kitchen and checked the thermometer outside. It read a blistering eighty-nine degrees in the shade. *Ugh!* When I turned around to help Jeff in the kitchen, I saw a gorgeous green watermelon sitting on the counter. If painted orange, it would have made a beautiful jack-o-lantern.

"Wow! That's a beaut!" I commented.

"You know how much I paid for that thing?" Jeff quizzed.

Uh, oh. Suddenly, I was a contestant in Jeff's "Guess the Price of this Produce" game. I bit and said, "Five bucks."

"Nope," he said, "four bucks. You know how much it was all cut up in a bowl about this size?" My husband held his hands around an imaginary bowl.

"Six dollars?" I guessed, taking a wild shot in the dark.

"Nope, nine dollars. Can you believe it?" He exclaimed.

Holy crap! I thought to myself. *That is one expensive carving job.* The news just reaffirmed my faith in my husband and in his budget-conscious management skills. I opened up the refrigerator to put away the rest of the produce, meat and dairy products, and a cool blast of chilled air greeted me. Even better, two large bottles of chardonnay caught my attention from the bottom shelf. I howled with laughter and spun around to face Jeff. "Thank you, for buying me, not one, but two doses of mother's helper!"

Jeff smiled. "It's in honor of Carolyn, and hopefully they should last you through the week—or at least through Wednesday!"

"Ha! Ha!" I rolled my eyes.

The rest of the conscientiously purchased grocery items were unpacked from the green and black recycling bags. We made a bite to eat for lunch and sat down at the kitchen table. Jeff took my hand in his, and we bowed our heads and offered a prayer for our many blessings, for Carolyn, for Dorothy and her family, for our loved ones, and for the military troops who had served and were still serving at home and abroad to protect our freedoms and our great country on that Memorial Day weekend.

Amen.

CHAPTER 15

Shades of Red

Ring. Ring. Buzz. Buzz. Ding. Ding.

The DGs' phones perpetually rang and vibrated; their emails and texts dinged throughout the Memorial Day weekend. All forms of communication ping-ponged back and forth among DGs discussing a whole host of details: determining what would be the optimal day to bring dinner over to Dorothy's house; reviewing types of casseroles; inquiring about food preferences; confirming there were no food allergies concerning the kids; planning funeral attire; scheduling hair appointments, manicures and pedicures.

Since it was a three-day holiday weekend, Dorothy suggested Monday afternoon for the DGs to bring over dinner and spend some time together. Margaret and her two children would also be included, having arrived in Georgia from Texas by then. As the point person coordinating the menu, I enlisted Jeff's mom, Alayne. She decided to make the main dish—white lasagna with an Alfredo sauce. Having enjoyed it on numerous occasions over the years, I knew the freezable casserole was not only hearty and delicious, but also smelled divine when the garlic, basil, oregano, spicy Italian sausage, chopped marinated red peppers, and ricotta and mozzarella cheeses were baking in the oven. The recipe even called for one-fourth cup of mother's helper, so no wonder Alayne prepared this signature dish for company!

"I'll drop it off at your house on Monday afternoon when I'm out running errands," Alayne said during our phone conversation.

"Perfect," I told her. "Thank you! Doing that will be a timesaver."

Susie and Carole had planned to meet at my house so we could ride to Dorothy's together, but in the meantime I needed to get organized. Pulling out a scratch piece of paper and an ink pen from my desk in the kitchen, and also grabbing a phone, I sat at the table and made a list for the full menu. As each DG I called took responsibility for something to bring, I checked it off: Susie, fresh vegetable and fruit trays; Carole, garlic bread and a chopped garden salad. With all but the most important food groups covered, I decided to make Rice Krispies Treats topped with a melted blend of chocolate and butterscotch morsels. The kids would devour them in seconds and all of the DG loved chocolate. I also felt that bottles of mother's helper and father's helper were in order for Dorothy and Robert, and added the adult beverage to my name. My task was completed.

Check. Done. Move on.

Susie and I also scheduled our manicures and pedicures together at a local nail salon on Monday morning at ten, granting her plenty of time to sleep in. It was not uncommon for her to watch movies into the wee hours of the morning or post updates to Facebook at ungodly times. A night owl through and through, she cherished the last day of any holiday weekend and dreaded the thought of having to set the alarm clock again for 6:00 A.M. No shocker, then, that I saw no sign of Susie's light blue Toyota Camry in the parking lot of the salon when I arrived on time!

"Chào!" I called to the ladies in the salon. Chào, pronounced, *ja-ow*, is a Vietnamese greeting for any time of day. In my Southern mind, I was simply saying *hey*—in Vietnamese! Since going to that salon, I'd asked the Vietnamese-American nail technicians to teach me a little of their native language. In turn, I would help them with their English. I found the intonations of Vietnamese fascinating and loved to listen as they spoke with one another. We were mutually adapting to the multicultural community we shared and broadening our experiences.

"Chào, Ms. Katie," greeted Hanna, a petite woman with black bobbed hair. "You, come sit over here." She pointed towards one of the empty massage chairs. The foot basin contained swirling, blue water that smelled of lavender.

"My friend Susie is also coming over here this morning to get her nails and toes polished," I announced, rolling up my pant legs. I sat in the vibrating chair and slowly submerged my feet into the luxurious, warm water. Leaning my head back, I closed my eyes.

Ahhh, this is heavenly.

Fifteen minutes passed before I heard the front door ding-dong. Evidently, Susie had simply rolled out of bed, down the stairs and into the car in order to meet me before the lunch hour. Her hair was uncombed and pulled back into a ponytail. She wore no makeup, and pillowcase markings left a wrinkled impression on her left cheek.

I giggled at her as she climbed into the chair next to me. Susie pressed the button to power her seat forward while vigorously kicking her feet until they came in contact with footrests.

"Oh, shut up, you!" Susie joked. She bent over to roll up one of her pant legs, lost her balance and nearly fell into the bubbling foot bath, but was laughing at herself by the time Hanna had rushed over to steady her back into the chair.

"Miss Susie, you okay? Here, I do for you." Hanna finished rolling up the other pant leg as Susie settled in. The Susie Show, however, continued, and I watched in amusement. Her cheeks reddened as she frantically started punching the control buttons.

"*What* are you trying to do?" I leaned out of my chair to help her fix whatever dilemma she was experiencing.

"Geesh!" she exclaimed. "How do you stop the 'seat' mode for this massage chair? I'm getting rammed in the butt by something, and my butt cheeks are being squeezed together." Susie squirmed about, creating more red in her face. Remarkably, the heat in her face cheeks had seared the pillow wrinkles right out!

"Here, I'll make it stop, or would you like the sensation intensified?" I winked at her, raising and lowering my eyebrows.

"Heaven's no! Just … make … it … stop," she said through gritted teeth and an uncontrollable grin. Susie then burst out laughing and slapped my hand just as I found the "off" mode that put an end to her memorable experience.

"What color would you like today, girls?" Hanna asked on her way to a display with rows and rows of every nail polish color imaginable.

Susie and I looked at each other and then back to Hanna. "Red," we said in unison.

Hanna pulled shades of red ranging from orange to bluish.

"Here, this one is perfect for us," I said, pointing to the one.

"Dep. Cám ơn," Hanna replied, meaning *pretty* and *thank you*.

Susie agreed. The polish was the perfect color: a classic 1950's flat red that Carolyn would wear and absolutely approve. Wearing it would be a fitting tribute to her.

CHAPTER 16

Girls Just Want to Have Fun

Susie and I finished our manicures and pedicures, and temporarily went our separate ways. In the meantime, I returned home. Jeff's mom dropped off the casserole and reiterated the baking instructions, which I already knew by heart.

Carole and Susie then arrived so we could drive to Dorothy's together. During the ride over, Susie and I filled in Carole about our morning escapades and listened to eighties' music. When I pulled into Dorothy's driveway, we were singing Cyndi Lauper's, "Girls Just Want to Have Fun" at the top of our lungs and dancing around in our seats. Songs from the eighties magically transported us back to our days of youth. We were acting like fifteen-year-old teenagers disguised in forty-seven-year-old bodies.

Still singing, we vacated the car in a procession up the front walkway with food trays, fruit baskets and grocery bags. My mood shifted, however, when I noticed the change in the gardenia bush. No longer fragrant, the blossoms had yellowed and withered on the stems. Some petals had fallen off onto the pine straw bed below.

Margaret greeted us at the door. Younger but at least five inches taller than her sister Dorothy, she leaned over to hug each one of us as we entered the house. We made our way back to the kitchen, where Dorothy greeted us. Robert and the kids were sitting in the den, captivated by a show about antique cars.

While the television blared in the background, we unloaded and stored the four-course meal in the refrigerator. In the event that I was knocked unconscious or suffered an acute case of amnesia on the way to Dorothy's house, Jeff's mom had written the cooking instructions for the freezable casserole on a white index card and taped it to the foil covering the ceramic dish. I retrieved the bottles of mother's and father's helper, and ceremoniously carried the latter, Scotch, with both hands to the den. Robert was in his favorite brown leather recliner.

"Ta da! Here," I said, handing the bottle over to him and bowing in a grand gesture. "This is for you from Jeff and me."

"Ah, this is just what the doctor ordered," Robert said. "Awesome! Thank you!" He sat the bottle next to him on the side table.

Pop!

The sound of a wine bottle being uncorked, followed by the clatter of glasses on the granite countertop, beckoned me back to the kitchen. After quickly hugging the kids, I returned to the girls. Dorothy had opened a chilled bottle of chardonnay for us, so with the beverage in hand, we gathered around the kitchen table. The red tablecloth from the graduation party had been removed. There were no signs of the hospice brochures or the medication notebook. The house had been cleaned.

"Toast," I offered, raising my glass into the air. The rest of the girls followed suit. "To Carolyn. May the angels be with her! She is now with God in heaven and at peace."

"Here! Here! Cheers! To Carolyn! We love you, Carolyn!" different ones answered.

We made our glasses clink and took a sip. The wine was good—dry and spicy with an oak undertone. Breaking from our usual workday ruts and weekly routines, imbibing on a Monday afternoon made us feel a bit indulgent, like eating dessert before dinner. Simply scandalous!

Stories unfolded one by one around the table. Dorothy took the lead, recapping the events from the past few days and describing in detail how she and Margaret toiled over the clothes in Carolyn's closet for the right funeral outfit. They didn't want their mom to haunt them for making a fashion faux pas! Carole relayed Susie and my nail salon story in such perfect detail that you would have thought she'd seen it all firsthand rather than having had heard about it later in the car. Susie and I showed off our newly manicured nails and toes, polished in "Carolyn" red.

"Oh, my gosh!" Margaret and Dorothy exclaimed in unison. "We did the exact same thing, too!" Dorothy said. "How funny!" The two sisters flaunted their recently painted red finger and toenails, also done in homage to their mother.

"Well, I guess I know what I'm doing when I get home tonight," Carole interjected, indicating she was not going to be the only DG without red nails and toes to commemorate Carolyn at the funeral on Wednesday.

We bantered back and forth. Wine glasses emptied pretty quickly, so Dorothy poured us another round as we reminisced days gone by.

"Oh, remember that time when we all went to Daytona Beach on spring break and took Margaret with us?" Carole blurted out.

Margaret had become an adopted DG during her college years, after Dorothy married. We took her under our wings and invited her on weekend road trips and vacation getaways. Single, poor, anxious to get away from the nursing textbooks and classes, and head to the beach, I had asked Carole to research places to stay in Florida. I'd known she'd find us the best—or most affordable—vacation deal. The year was 19-something, B.G.—Before Google. Relying on books we found in the bookstore's travel section and brochures we requested by mail, we zeroed in on Daytona Beach—an ideal location with only a ninety-minute drive inland to Epcot.

The AAA travel guide indicated that the Robin Hood Motel located on N. Atlantic Avenue was an utter bargain that could accommodate Carole, Susie, Susan, Margaret and me for the week, even during spring break. Most importantly, it met our sparse budget requirements. We decided that we could afford a one-room unit with two double beds. The pullout cot would be for Susie, who preferred to sleep solo. The efficiency rooms also came complete with their own kitchenettes. According to Carole, we could conserve our money by making our own breakfasts and lunches. We'd splurge on dinners, Epcot, nightclubs and dancing.

The grand plan, adopted by all, was executed with tremendous anticipation. When we saw the actual Robin Hood Motel, which was located just down the street from the Peter Pan Motel, however, we got the sense that the promotional literature had told a little fairytale.

"That place was so old and outdated!" Susie blurted out, cringing as the vintage décor reemerged from the memory banks in her head.

The circa 1950's efficiency motel, located "Directly on the World's Most Famous Beach," as advertised on the back of their postcards, succeeded in meeting our basic Maslow's physiological need for shelter—period.

"Gosh! Remember how small that cinderblock room was with all five of us?" I said, shaking my head at the thought of it.

The room was so tiny that we had to push the twin beds together to accommodate Susie's cot. To enter the bathroom, we had to climb over the cot. A leap off the end of one of the double beds landed you in the one-person kitchenette. Miraculously, a refrigerator, sink, microwave and toaster oven had all fit in the space. And it's a good thing we had a kitchen sink to serve as a spare basin for washing our hair when the line for the shower backed up.

The room's other alleged amenities either didn't work or worked overtime. Susie's morning routine of warming her pastries in the toaster oven consistently set off the smoke alarm in the room. To clear the smoke, we'd dance around like my mom who put out fires in her kitchen by swirling a dish towel over our heads. When that didn't work, we'd shove the twin beds aside to open the door—and only safe exit.

"It was so cramped, but we didn't care," Susie said. "And, do you remember that seafood restaurant we ate at one night?" She punched Carole's arm to jog her memory.

We laughed knowing that Carole didn't need a punch in the arm to remember every last detail of that event. Anyway, we would never have let her forget it as long as we lived and could remember to tell the tale:

"Carole, you found a coupon in one of the local travel magazines for a 'buy one dinner, get one free' for an 'all-you-can-eat' seafood buffet a few streets over," Susie said. "The catch was that the coupon was only good between the hours of 4:00 and 6:00 P.M."

"Ah," I interjected, "that should have been a clue for us, but no-o-o! We dressed up in our preppy madras shirts, skirts or white Bermuda shorts, pink sweater vests, and, of course, our gold add-a-bead necklaces, and set out at 3:45 for our fine dining experience. And who else was clamoring to get through the front door of the place? A sea of elderly people with wheelchairs, walkers and canes! When we finally made our way to the cashier stand, the hostess gave us such a funny look. She set us at a table for five anyway. Little did we know that the restaurant served as the cafeteria for the retirement center in the same building directly above, and we were taking part in their early-bird special!"

Margaret pointed across the table at Carole and shook her finger at her. "You! You and your brilliant cost-saving ideas!" The group erupted into spontaneous laughter.

"You know, we made their night," Carole chided back.

"Oh, I am sure we did," I replied.

Our hopes and dreams of running into a group of single, young, collegiate men on their spring break evaporated the moment we realized that the average age in the place was eighty-five. In true DG fashion, nonetheless, we adapted to the situation at hand, made the absolute best of it, and had such a great time mixing and mingling with the elderly crowd! The men and women wanted to know everything about us: Why are you here? Where are you from? What are you studying in college? What do you want to be when you grow up? Likewise, when we went up to the buffet, we helped them fill their plates and offered them assistance back to their seats. There was no denying that they were incredibly darling companions on that late afternoon.

"Oh, and remember all of the practical jokes we played on each other during that trip?" Margaret said during a light bulb moment.

"Yes, yes, I do!" I exclaimed. My Cheshire cat grin appeared. I was notorious for being at the epicenter of all pranks. "On the road trip down to Daytona," I shared, "Margaret, Carole and I got bored sitting in the back seat together. As a form of amusement, we found some extra paper in the car and scribbled, 'Honk, if you like sex!' We placed the sign in the back window of Susie's car, out of her line of sight. For miles and miles, cars and trucks honked and waved at us. Susie thought she was driving on the friendliest roads through most welcoming towns."

"Yea, it wasn't until we'd stopped for gas and I walked around the rear of the car did I notice their sign in the window!" Susie sputtered, wiping tears from her eyes. Her face was beet red from laughing.

Susie ripped that sign from the window, tore it into a million pieces, and threw it into the garbage can by the gas pump. She then swore she'd get even with us. Remembering had us laughing as hard as we'd laughed about it then.

"And poor Margaret!" I added. "One night, when Margaret had fallen asleep before the rest of us, we placed all of her bras in a plastic sealable bag that we filled with water and stuck in the freezer. When she noticed they were missing the next morning, we sent her on a scavenger hunt through the room to find them." I leaned over to Margaret and patted her on the back; she was also wiping away tears from her face.

"I had to thaw them in hot water and chip my bras out of the bag with a fork," Margaret reminded us. "I hung them everywhere in the room to dry so I could wear one that day." Margaret leaned towards me and popped me on the back of the head, knowing I initiated the prank from the start.

"My stomach aches from laughing so much," I said. "This has been a great way to spend the afternoon." I rubbed my belly and checked my watch. Time was slipping away and rapidly approaching the supper hour. "Hey, we better get a move on so you can have your dinner," I declared. "Did you say the minister was coming over later tonight to go over last-minute funeral and ceremony details?"

"Oh, my! Is it getting to be that late?" Dorothy wondered. "Yes, he is coming over at 7:30 this evening." We all got up from the table, returned our empty wine glasses to the sink and headed for the front door. After hugging and kissing Dorothy's family good-bye, Carole, Susie and I piled into the car and headed for home.

In two days, the DGs would gather again; Carolyn's funeral was Wednesday.

CHAPTER 17
The Angel on Earth

Despite all of the preparation for Carolyn's funeral, Wednesday seemed to arrive in the blink of an eye.

On that bright, blue sky morning, I decided to wear one of my black suits. (Jeff vacillated between navy versus black, ultimately choosing black, too.) I slipped on a pair of black, patent leather mules so the open toes of the shoes would showcase my "Carolyn" red toenail polish. With my outfit and hair in place, I sat at bathroom vanity to take my time putting on my makeup. I was being slow and methodical, thoughtfully picking out the right shades of blush, eye shadows and eyeliners. To make my last vital decision, the lipstick shade for the day, I rummaged through my cosmetic drawer, taking the tops off each tube to find the perfect color—a "Carolyn" matte red. Finding the one, I lined my lips with a taupe-brown pencil to prevent the red from bleeding across the vermilion boarder, and filled in my upper and lower lips with the lipstick using a lip brush. For the finishing touch, I gently pressed my lips against a piece of tissue to blot and seal in the color. I glanced in the mirror above the sink for one final assessment before exiting the bathroom: perfect!

Carole, Kurt and Susie wanted to carpool down to Patterson's Funeral Home together, so we agreed to have everyone gather at our home and depart from there. As expected, Carole and Kurt were the first to arrive, but Susie wasn't late. She appeared within ten minutes, although she was in a rush with flecks of tan powder on her shirt. I brushed them off her shoulders while she went on about applying her makeup in the car to keep herself on time.

Jeff was our designated driver, so Kurt climbed into the front passenger seat and shouted, "Shotgun!" Susie sat sandwiched between Carole and me in the back. During the thirty-minute car ride down I-85 South to the funeral home, the men gabbed away about sports and recent news events until Kurt asked about Jeff's work at the police department.

"What is your most memorable moment as a police officer?" Kurt inquired.

Great question, I thought. Jeff issued a long pause. I could tell he was mulling over the question, sifting through a myriad of events over his twenty-five year career for the one event that stood out from the rest. I couldn't let the pause go too long and interrupted, "Our wedding night!"

It was obvious that everyone had been waiting with baited breath to hear Jeff reveal some scary, gruesome story or a heroic tale, so my unforeseen comment caused spontaneous howls of laughter. I thought the car windows would shatter!

After Jeff regained control of the steering wheel, he uttered, "I can't top that answer—at all!"

A reverent silence descended among us when we arrived at H.M. Patterson & Son Funeral Home. I could understand why Carolyn had to wait a few days for her funeral. The parking lot was packed with cars and people were emerging from all directions. Jeff drove up to the front entrance to let the three DGs out of the car, and the two men circled the lots to find a parking spot.

We solemnly waited for the guys in the vestibule before entering the Oglethorpe Hill Chapel as a group. The last time I had been in that very room was thirteen years earlier for Dorothy's father's funeral. We proceeded to guest registry, which we signed, and collected Carolyn's memorial card before searching for Dorothy and Margaret. Family from Tennessee and other relatives, neighbors from the subdivision, Angel Flight staff and volunteers, and Dorothy's coworkers filled the holding area in the back of the chapel. A video montage of photographs taken of Carolyn over the course of her lifetime played, and a small crowd of people had gathered to watch. Religious music played quietly through the overhead speakers.

We spotted Dorothy and Margaret welcoming guests and caught their attention. The two made their way over to the small conversational circle that we had formed, and when they joined the intimate ring, a group hug commenced.

Upon looking down, Dorothy was the first to realize that she, Margaret, Carole, Susie and I were all wearing open-toed shoes and sporting our "Carolyn" red polish. "Oh, look at us!" Dorothy exclaimed, pointing her right foot into the center of the circle. The rest of the DGs followed her lead.

Jeff, without skipping a beat, put his hands on his hips, pointed his foot and thrust his wingtip into the middle with the rest of us. "And, I've had my toes painted, too!" Jeff mimicked in the best constrained DG voice he could muster.

As if on cue, we giggled—collectively, quietly and conservatively. We knew Carolyn was looking down on us, enjoying the tribute. I could, in that moment, hear her clapping her hands, laughing, and in her raspy voice, saying, Well done, girls! Well done!

"Where's Baynham?" Dorothy inquired.

"Not sure, we haven't heard or seen her yet," I said. "I know she's coming with her mom. I'm sure they'll be here shortly." I scoured the room for signs of Baynham and her mother, but didn't locate any evidence. While waiting, I approached the television showing pictures of Carolyn and recognized many, including my favorite black and white of her modeling the gorgeous black dress ensemble. Then, out of the corner of my eye, I saw Susan and her mom.

"Hey," I said, hugging Susan and Mrs. Baynham. "Good to see you both."

Susan looked flustered and bothered by something, and immediately vented. "We would have been here sooner, but when I was leaving to pick up Mom, I walked into the garage to find that my car had a flat tire. I called Mom and she had to rush to my house and pick me up." Baynham prided herself as a punctual person and hated arriving late to any event, but her stoic nature also masked her feelings of loss, so there was more to her crankiness than a flat tire.

Interrupting my response, a voice announced overhead, "Please be seated. We'll be starting the ceremony in just a few minutes. Please take your seats."

The conversational noise from the crowd lowered to a whisper, and the group formed two side-by-side single file lines. Walking down the center aisle of the chapel, everyone present filled the empty pews to the right and left. Once seated, I noted the variety of flower arrangements, including two identical potted flower gardens from the Smith and Hart families, displayed across the elevated chancel. A cross sat atop the altar. Carolyn's ashes, however, were not present for the memorial service. Dorothy had confided in me earlier that she had decided not to put Mom on exhibit. She just couldn't do it. The ceremony was hard enough on her and Margaret. Instead, keeping her cremated remains private, she and Margaret planned to release them in Tennessee at a later date.

Dorothy, Margaret and the remainder of the family were the last to be ushered into the chapel. They proceeded down the aisle in complete silence, taking their seats in the pews a few rows directly in front of us.

The ministers from Dorothy's local Methodist church provided the eulogy. Listening to her being referred to in a past tense was tough for the entire congregation, who loved and adored Carolyn. We wept quietly. The preachers highlighted the accomplishments in her life, her community volunteerism, and addressed her love of reading, cooking and decorating. The hardest part of the tribute to hear was that she left behind her two daughters and three grandchildren. That's when the reality and finality of her death set in. She was no longer with us in her earthly form, to laugh with, to talk with, to joke with and to visit with anymore.

However, mourning Carolyn's death also reminded us to take the time to celebrate her life. What remained within each one of our hearts was her jovial spirit, her love and the cherished memories of her. While in our hearts, she was His angel on earth. In awe of God's glory, I was overcome by a sense of peace and acceptance.

Amen.

CHAPTER 18
Prayers Answered

Ring. Ring. Buzz. Buzz. Ding. Ding.

The DG's phones perpetually rang and vibrated, while emails and text messages dinged. It was the week before the thirtieth-year reunion of our Dunwoody High School graduating class. We were the Class of 1982.

All forms of communication ping-ponged back and forth between and among the DGs as we discussed a whole host of details: determining the appropriate snack foods and drinks for the social reception; confirming our block of rooms located next door to each other in the hotel; deciding what clothes to bring; planning party attire and lending out jewelry; scheduling hair appointments, manicures and pedicures.

On that momentous Friday night in June, the once again DGs gathered to celebrate, commemorate and connect with old friends. Dorothy, well-rested, was in the process of finalizing her mom's estate and ready to let her hair down. She was adapting and beginning a new chapter in her life, one without Carolyn.

We were all changed from losing another DG mom, but the bonds we all shared were constant, and for the next three days, the DGs were inseparable, just like old times. I returned home from the reunion weekend with a sense of renewal, empowerment and fearlessness. I was ready to conquer the world once more.

During the weekend, I had a great time reconnecting with old classmates, and with the power of Facebook, looked forward to staying in touch with them long after the festivities. I would begin by posting pictures of our reunion. While capturing numerous photos over the course of the celebration, I made sure that the DGs reenacted an old pose shown in a picture taken of us over thirty years earlier, when we were still in high school, by my sister.

Back home in my basement office, I downloaded the reunion photos to my laptop. Clicking through the frames, I looked for that one snapshot. Finding it, I searched through my electronic photo files for the one taken of us as kids. With a little editing, I posted them side-by-side. Relishing the moment, I sat back in my chair, comparing the girls with the innocent, baby expressions on the left with the wise, appropriately aged faces on the right.

Carolyn had always advised to let go and have fun in life no matter where the journey led, and boy, did we ever! If those two groups could turn and face each other with the older DGs bearing witness to the younger ones about what life had in store for them over the next thirty years, nothing—absolutely nothing—could be said to prepare the girls for the divine journey they were embarking on together. Or for the racing hours, days, months and years!

Moments in time had passed so quickly, but we had made each moment count. Our lives were a collection of our experiences and our relationships with one another and with our parents. Along the way, we had faced challenges together that shaped who we had become today. Ultimately, the difficulties defined us, creating strong, beautiful and independent Southern women. We were Carolyn's dream fulfilled. We were the DGs, ready to report for duty at a moment's notice.

Carolyn's life lessons had been pearls of wisdom that I collected, cherished and treasured. From her more than anyone, I learned to listen to my heart, follow my dreams and open my heart to love. More importantly, she would become a constant reminder that life was all about love—giving and receiving it.

She always said that it was a rare thing to have lifelong girlfriends and that the DGs' bond was special. Eventually, she asked me to make sure that I continued to look after the girls as I had done all my life. Without any hesitation, I'd promised her that I would and that we'd always be there for each other, even after our parents were gone.

She taught me that I was free to live my own life and make my own choices. I was accountable for my actions, too.

Couch Time with Carolyn sessions prepared me to be a better person. They challenged me to rebuild, grow and persevere through life no matter what it threw at me, and taking the lessons to heart, I awakened to evolve and realize my full potential, blooming into the woman I knew God had planned for me to be.

Sometimes life tests you. You don't get a study guide or a warning that it's coming. You have to be able to stand on your own. It's pass or fail. Ultimately, the choices you make determine the direction you will go.

I could only imagine what the next thirty years had in store for us. I planned to let go, throw my hands up in the air and just enjoy the ride.

Alone in my office, I rested my head on my chair and closed my eyes. It wasn't hard to envision Carolyn holding court from her favorite chair in her den, her legs outstretched on the ottoman. I could also see the DGs side by side on the yellow sofa, each holding a glass of mother's helper.

In my daydream, Carolyn raises a glass of chardonnay in her left hand and holds her cigarette between her right index and middle fingers. Stale smoke hovers in the air as Carolyn, in her best Southern drawl, tells us, "Girls, each day brings a new adventure. Embrace it. Life will test you. Pass it. Keep your heads held high! Walk through life with style and grace. Wear your red lipstick with your finger and toe nails polished red, too! Cheers to you!" A group toast commences, and, of course, we all take a sip from our glasses before setting them back down—*for good luck.* And we feel the common thread that binds us through life: *love.*

After all, isn't that what it's all about anyway?

Before I closed my eyes that night to go to sleep, I kissed Jeff and said a prayer.

Dear God,

I am no longer divorced, lost, or afraid. I have more than forty dollars in my checking account, and I will work to help sustain others this week. I pray that you will watch over Jeff and me. Keep us safe from harm. Allow us to be your ever faithful servants. While the road ahead is uncertain, my true love and I will walk it together with you. Please bless and care for my family and friends. Forgive me for my sins. Please let me walk in your world for another day so that I can continue to be the woman you created me to be.

Your faithful servant,

Katie

P. S. Go Dawgs!

In your name I pray. Amen.

The Dunwoody Girl's

Scrapbook

Carole, Dorothy, Susie, Susan, Katie & Margaret (L to R)

1980

Carolyn Sewell

Carolyn in her

high school years

Carolyn's

modeling days

Carolyn Sewell

Carolyn wearing her 4th of July Hat

Carolyn wearing her 4th of July Hat

Carolyn was known by her grandchildren as "Nan Nan"

The Hart Family

My parents

My early years in San Diego, CA

Hart Family Christmas

(Mom wearing her signature pearl necklace!)

The Hart Family

Grandma Gigi

"A total spit fire!"

Uncle Bill taking Julie and

I under his wings

Cousin Emily and I celebrate

milestone birthdays together

at Hart Family Reunions

The Dunwoody Girls

Dunwoody United Methodist
Church Youth Choir Tour Trip

Dorothy, Mom, Me & Susie (L to R)

Spring Break trip to
Daytona Beach, FL

The Dunwoody Girls

The DG's trip to Disney's Epcot Theme Park

Baynham, Susie, Margaret, Carole and I (L to R)

Baynham and I looking
for our Knight in Shining
Armor – this guy was a
bit hollow and quiet.

Heading out to the "All You Can
Eat" Seafood Buffet

The Dunwoody Girls

Jumpin' for Joy!

Spring Break to Panama City Beach, FL

Carole in the Atlanta All
Women's Road Rally

Baynham and I seeking
out adventures while
single in the city

The Dunwoody Girls

Dunwoody High School Class
of 1982

Our 10th Year Reunion

Dorothy and I in 1980 (L)
and at the DHS 25yr
Reunion Party (R)

The DGs attending the DHS
30th Reunion in 2012

Carolyn and her girls

"Girls, each day brings a new adventure. Embrace it. Life will test you. Pass it. Keep your heads held high! Walk through life with style and grace. Wear your red lipstick with your finger and toe nails polished red, too! Cheers to you!"

1980   2012

In Memory of

Carolyn H. Sewell

March 12, 1927 - May 25, 2012

About The Author

With over 20 years of experience, Katie Hart Smith has written for a wide array of audiences. Smith's literary work ranges from medical and academic publications to children's stories.

Smith loved writing as a child, creating her own story and picture books at an early age. As a young adult, she pursued a nursing career and in 1987 obtained a B.S. in Nursing from Georgia State University. In 2002, she received a MBA from Troy State University. Throughout her professional career, she continued to write for the medical community. In 1995, Smith published her first memoir, "In the Face of Disaster: Personal Reflections" that was published as an article in the *Orthopaedic Nursing* Journal.

A former City Council member for the City of Lawrenceville, she remains an active member and volunteer in her community. Smith, her husband, Jeff, and their three furry, four-legged kids reside in Lawrenceville, Georgia.

For more information about Smith, her "From the Heart" blog, and for a complete publication listing, visit:
www.katiehartsmith.com.